*To Pray and
to Love*

Roberta C. Bondi

To Pray & to Love

Conversations on Prayer
with the Early Church

Fortress Press   Minneapolis

BV207
.B66
1991

23386 462

TO PRAY AND TO LOVE

Cover design: Carol Evans-Smith

Library of Congress Cataloging-in-Publication Data

Bondi, Roberta C.
    To pray and to love : conversations on prayer with the early
church / Roberta C. Bondi.
        p.   cm.
    Includes bibliographical references and index.
    ISBN 0-8006-2511-0
    1. Prayer—Christianity—History—Early church, ca. 30-600.
2. Prayer.   3. Christian life—1960-   I. Title.
BV207.B66   1991
248.3'2'09015—dc20   91-3026
                                                                    CIP

The paper used in this publication meets the minimum requirements of American National Standard for Information Sciences—Permanence of Paper for Printed Library Materials, ANSI Z329.48-1984.   ∞™

Manufactured in the U.S.A.   AF 1-2511
95   94   93   92   91   1   2   3   4   5   6   7   8   9   10

Contents

Acknowledgments

Many people have contributed to the writing of this book. I would like especially to thank those who read all or parts of the manuscript and who not only gave suggestions but also real encouragement and support while I was writing it: Joanna Adams, Leslie Akin, Walter Brueggemann, Pam Couture, Rebecca Chopp, Vicki Laughlin Gary, Rod Hunter, Martin Iott, O. P., Bill Mallard, Nicole Mills, Carol Newsom, Nancy Sehested, Jan Stephens.

I owe a special thanks to my colleague Don Saliers who originally encouraged me in the writing of this book and who was the first to read the completed manuscript.

Alan Gregory made particularly helpful suggestions for the final revision of this manuscript and I am very grateful to him.

Gail O'Day was also there with encouragement at the first and at the last and all the time in between.

Melissa Walker, my friend of so many years, supported me in innumerable ways, including taking the picture for this book.

Marshall Johnson was a helpful and encouraging editor at Fortress Press.

Candler School of Theology gave me a house leave in the spring of 1987 to work on this book, and I appreciate it very much.

Benjamin, my son, was fun to live with and so lightened my task.

Nick, Romana, and Julius, my three cats, did not so much seek to help as to interfere, and I congratulate them that they were often somewhat successful, especially in the matter of paws on the keyboard.

Most of all, I thank my husband Richard. He was a constant conversation partner who always had good insights into the problems with which I was dealing. He also cooked me good meals, comforted me when I was discouraged, and made me laugh.

Chapter 1

"Pray without Ceasing"

*P*aul tells us, "Pray without ceasing." What does Paul mean by this, and how ought we to pray? For the desert fathers and mothers of the early church, the right answers to these questions depend upon the needs and personality of the person asking the question. Consider these three very different images of prayer.

> Abba Macarius was asked, "How should one pray?" The old man said, "There is no need at all to make long discourses; it is enough to stretch out one's hands and say, 'Lord, as you will, and as you know, have mercy.' And if the conflict grows fierce say, 'Lord, help!' [God] knows very well what we need and [God] shews us [God's] mercy."[1]

For Abba Macarius prayer would appear to be a simple, straightforward asking for God's help in the face of temptation. Abba Joseph, however, in the following saying, gives—and demonstrates—very different advice to one of his disciples, who was also a teacher of prayer.

> Abba Lot went to see Abba Joseph and said to him, "Abba, as far as I can, I say my little office, I fast a little, I pray and meditate, I live in peace and as far as I can, I purify my thoughts. What else can I do?" Then the old man stood up and stretched his hands toward heaven. His fingers became like ten lamps of fire and he said to him, "If you will, you can become all flame."[2]

Abba Lucius, confronted by monks who understood Paul's advice in a way that was both literal and simpleminded, presents us with a third way of prayer:

> Some of the monks who are called Euchites went . . . to see Abba Lucius. The old man asked them, "What is your manual work?" They said, "We

do not touch manual work but as the Apostle says, we pray without ceasing." The old man asked them if they did not eat and they replied that they did. So he said to them, "When you are eating, who prays for you then?" Again, he asked them if they did not sleep and they replied that they did. And he said to them, "When you are asleep, who prays for you then?" They could not find any answer to give him. He said to them, "Forgive me, but you do not act as you speak. I will show you how, while doing my manual work, I pray without interruption. I sit down with God, soaking my reeds and plaiting my ropes, and I say, 'God have mercy on me; according to your great goodness and according to the multitude of your mercies, save me from my sins.' " So he asked them if this were not prayer and they replied it was. Then he said to them, "So when I have spent the whole day working and praying, making thirteen pieces of money more or less, I put two pieces of money outside the door and I pay for my food with the rest of the money. He who takes the two pieces of money prays for me when I am eating and when I am sleeping; so, by the grace of God, I fulfil the precept to pray without ceasing."[3]

For Abba Lucius, when we wish to speak of prayer without ceasing, even defining the boundary between our prayer and the prayer of another is not necessarily a straightforward matter. Nor does Lucius want to make a separation between the act and content of prayer and the work a monk does to provide for the needs of others who cannot care for themselves. For him prayer is a way of life that begins and ends in love.

What do we who would follow in the steps of Christians who have prayed before us hear Paul asking us to do when he tells us, "Pray without ceasing"? What is prayer for us, and what could it mean for us to pray unceasingly?

For most of us who have grown up without a tradition of private prayer that goes beyond reciting "Now I lay me . . ." and the Lord's Prayer, or praying for a specific need in a particular situation, the whole subject of prayer can be baffling and painful. We do not know what prayer ought to be; we cannot quite seize hold of how to think about it, and we suspect it may not even be justifiable if it involves asking God to change what already is. We are used to the public prayer of worship services, but private prayer is another matter. We may have been turned away from the idea of private prayer by people we know whose piety is so individualistic that they refuse to believe Christians have any real social responsibility for the world and its people. We may associate prayer and people who talk about it with self-righteousness, religious fanaticism, or a blameworthy innocence about what the nature of the world is. Depending upon our church and family traditions, there is a good possibility that we believe it is not even polite to talk about prayer.

In spite of all this, many people have a real longing for prayer. Perhaps our lives have been touched at a deep level by particular men and women we know who have been made who they are by their prayer. Some of us seek God in situations of moral ambiguity we cannot sort out but suspect we might be able to understand in prayer. Or it may be that a particular experience of worship has made us aware of a desire for prayer. Some people find that this longing has been awakened by a strong encounter with God. Others experience a desire for prayer as a kind of empty restlessness that makes God seem far away.

Many other people do pray regularly. Some have grown up in traditions in which private prayer is taken for granted; some have discovered prayer on their own, almost in spite of their tradition. Some regularly read books on prayer and some do not. In spite of all these ways of coming to prayer, however, many praying Christians have one thing in common: they lack confidence in their prayer. Even though they may pray daily, in many cases enjoying a deep relationship with God, they believe that they are not praying "right." Somehow they have become convinced that they ought to be praying harder, or more unselfishly, or with more concentration, or with more faith, or more systematically, or in a more centered way. Some of them are truly demoralized about prayer, as much as they want it; others feel vaguely guilty; still others, sad.

Finally, there are people whose experience of prayer is blessedly happy. Whether we learned to pray as children or as adults, from others or by ourselves, prayer is now as natural and unproblematic for us as breathing and eating. Perhaps we now have children or friends who are asking us about the prayer that has always come easily. It could be that we now desire to grow even more fully into a life of prayer with God with a special urgency under the pressure of important life changes: the birth of a child; the death of a family member or friend; a change in job or status; a serious illness. We may feel the need to think in a new way about our lives and our prayer.

It is for all of you who want to pray but do not know how, who pray but feel uncertain about it, and who pray happily but want to grow more deeply in it that this book has been written.

For those who have a longing for prayer and yet have never prayed, I will offer some specific suggestions, not so much about ways of prayer—this is not really a "how to" book—as about attitudes, beliefs, and dispositions that get in the way of our prayer without us even noticing. At the same time I hope to explore with you new ways of looking at what we do when we pray, for example: how Scripture is a part of our prayer; where intercessory prayer fits in; and spending time in silence in God's presence.

For those who pray but are discouraged or dissatisfied with prayer, I hope to open to you new ways of understanding prayer that will help you to have confidence and even joy in the prayer you have. I want to do this in part by helping you understand and believe in your hearts that because prayer is a shared life with God, what you may be interpreting as failure is probably simply a part of a long process of discovery. Prayer is different at different times in our lives. Sometimes we are full of joy and confidence with respect to our prayer. Sometimes prayer is a drudgery; sometimes it puts us in a state of terrible turmoil as it raises issues we would rather not have raised. I hope in this book to help you see how and why this is true.

I hope, finally, that this book will also help those of you already happy in your prayer but wanting to continue to grow deeper in the life of prayer and in the knowledge and love of God and those images of God we human beings are. For you I wish that the book becomes a further means of exploration into the whole long journey of a life of praying and loving.

All this I hope to do by sharing some of what the founders of early monasticism had to say about prayer and Christian love that I have found especially helpful over the years. Not that the intent is to teach you to pray as a fourth-century Christian; the monastic teachers were firmly grounded in their own world and time as we must be. Rather I want to offer the following pages in the hope that you may find in them something useful for your own prayer, reflection, and life in the present. The teachers of the Egyptian desert understood in a particular way that prayer, our everyday lives, and Christian reflection are all of one piece. Wherever our place in the ongoing journey of prayer, these Christian ancestors offer us solid help, support, insight, and comfort.

At first glance the early monastics we will study look like an unlikely group from which to seek help concerning prayer in our period, especially for Protestants. Partly this is because we tend to believe that monks and nuns rejected or at least intended to escape the world, while we seek to live and find our salvation in that same world they attempted to escape. In actual fact they and we are not so different. The concerns that led our Christian ancestors to leave their lives "in the world" are also our concerns: about earning a living in a Christian fashion, about the temptations of family life that prevent love or destroy the self, about consumerism, about desire for power over others for its own sake.

Some, no doubt, really may have thought of themselves as escaping the world. Most, on the contrary, believed that the goal of the Christian life is love of God and love of neighbor. Prayer for them was the ground in which that love was to grow as well as the means of its growth. Our ancestors in the faith did not imagine that there could be Christian prayer unless it was grounded in the life of the person who prays. The reason, then, that these men and women left the world was to try to find out how to love and to pray and to put their full energies into what they were doing. They did not want to escape responsibility for their world—far from it!

Furthermore, they did not conceive of their lives in the desert as easy because they had left the things that diverted them from love, nor did they think of themselves as better than those still living under the constraints of ordinary life. They saw themselves instead as stripping off a lot of external hindrances to love in order to get to the real struggle that was with themselves. As the great Anthony, the founder and hero of this movement said,

> The [one] who abides in solitude and is quiet, is delivered from fighting three battles—those of hearing, speech, and sight. Then [that person] will have but one battle to fight—the battle of the heart.[4]

They learned so much about the battle of the heart in prayer and love that they are still able to teach a lot to us, who still have to battle our own hearts in spite of the differences in culture, time, and material goods.

These ancient teachers of prayer have been profoundly transforming of my own life over the years, and I believe they may be for you, too.[5] From them I have learned to think about prayer and to pray from a very different and much wider perspective than I was ever accustomed to, and in the process I have discovered that

prayer is broader, more inclusive, more painful, and more transforming than I had thought.

I have learned from them that prayer is the fundamental reality
of our lives as Christians. We are formed by our prayer as we find
our center in God because it is how we are made: "Our hearts are
restless till they find their rest in you, oh God," said our fourth-
century Christian ancestor Augustine. It shapes our actions, our
decisions, our emotions, our habits, and our hearts as we move
toward the love of God and the love of God's images, other people.

I have learned from the monastic teachers that prayer is a back
and forth movement between us and God in the whole of our lives,
between God's continual grace and our continual response. It is
also a movement between our receptivity and friendly silence in
God's presence and our continual reflection on the meaning of what
we learn about God, ourselves, and others from the experience of
our prayer as we grow in love.

I have learned that prayer is also a movement between us and
the whole Christian community, ancient and modern, as we learn
from it, critique it, find our feet in it, and are sustained by it. In
our local communities prayer is the undergirding of our worship,
our deep friendships, and sometimes even painful divisions. It
connects us with the larger community of living Christians around
the world whose lives are different from our own and who may
not on the surface even share a form of Christianity similar to ours.
Prayer also connects us with the body of Christ through the ages,
the "cloud of witnesses"[6] that continuously surrounds us, the
prayers of those Christians who lived before us and who have left
us the legacy of their prayers and insights.

I have learned that prayer also connects us with ourselves; it
is the link between our new selves that are always being transformed into God's loving image and our old selves with which we
must come to terms if we are to be transformed. By it we are able
to discover who we are and move toward who we are to become.
By it we become able to love, to care for the people who have been
entrusted to us: our immediate neighbor and our far neighbors in
the whole of God's world.

Perhaps most significantly the ancient teachers have taught me
not to be discouraged with my own prayer but to persist in it, for
prayer, like love, as a way of life is not something that comes to
us ready-made simply by deciding we want it. We learn it with the

help of the Holy Spirit over a lifetime by practicing it, pondering it, and using the resources, including Scripture, that other Christians have passed on to us.

In spite of all the monastic teachers have taught me, however, this book is not meant to be "all about prayer in the early church." We cannot simply step back into ancient times and teachings and make them our model just as they are. To begin, as we have already seen, there is no single teaching on prayer in the early church; on some very important points the early teachers of prayer differ among themselves.[7] Further, a great span of centuries separates us, and we are separated from them even more by the differences in our two cultures than by the time span. Again, some of what they say is irrelevant to us, and some of it might even be harmful if we tried to act on it.[8] Nevertheless, I have tried to bring to you some of their basic insights into prayer and present them in such a way that this book may be both helpful to you and faithful to their teaching.

This is also not a book that talks much about public prayer—not because public prayer is unimportant but because it is presupposed. Ancient Christians prayed publicly and privately, and in many respects we know more about their public than their private prayer. Most Christians in our time already participate in public prayer in regular worship services. These services may not be everything we would like, but they are there for us to participate in. The situation is not the same with private prayer. Most of us know much less about private prayer than public. Even though there should be no such thing as Christian prayer that is cut off from the life of the whole church, the focus of this book is on private prayer.

The starting point and the ending point of this book is the early monastic conviction that love of God and of neighbor is the goal of the Christian life. For our Christian forebears, only a person who loves is a fully functioning human being. Yet, because of the presence of sin in the world, loving as God intends for us does not come easily. Learning to love is, in fact, what the Christian life is about, and it is a lifetime's enterprise.

Prayer is a profoundly integral part of this enterprise of learning to love. Only a small part of our prayer, however, is sitting down every day and deliberately spending time with God as we read Scripture, listen to God's voice, try to make sense of our lives in God's presence, and pray for others. The desert fathers and mothers insisted that our prayer and our life must be all of a piece. This means that there are two other "parts" of prayer outside of time specifically set aside for prayer.

First, there is thinking and reflecting. Pondering what it would mean to love specific people in our lives, trying to understand what it is that gets in the way of our ability to love, studying what other Christians through the centuries have to tell us about love of God and neighbor, consciously choosing patterns of behavior we know are loving, thinking through what our religious experiences have to teach us about love—all this "thinking" is a fundamental part of our prayer.

Second, there is the development and practice of loving ways of being. Apologizing for our unwarranted irritability, going out of our way to listen carefully to what someone we do not care for is saying to us, bringing ourselves to overcome shyness, fear of failure, or rejection to follow our conscience, developing a sense of ourselves as more than the sum total of our own and other people's expectations of us, sharing ourselves and our resources with others—all this "doing" that moves us toward love and expresses love is also an absolutely necessary part of prayer. Because the early monastic teachers did not speak of the practices of prayer, reflection, and everyday Christian living in isolation from each other, you will also find them woven together in this book.

THE BEGINNINGS OF MONASTIC LIFE

Once, the brothers in the monastery of Dorotheos of Gaza forgot what they were about in the monastic life. Using an illustration to which we will return often in this book, Dorotheos reminded them.

> Suppose we were to take a compass and insert the point and draw the outline of a circle. The center point is the same distance from any point on the circumference. . . . Let us suppose that this circle is the world and that God is the center; the straight lines drawn from the circumference to the center are the lives of [human beings]. . . .

Let us assume for the sake of the analogy that to move toward God, then, human beings move from the circumference along the various radii of the circle to the center.

But at the same time, the closer they are to God, the closer they become to one another; and the closer they are to one another, the closer they become to God.[9]

For the early monastic teachers, love stands at the heart of the Christian life, as its starting point, its goal, and its content. This love was not an abstraction but a concrete part of their daily lives. In order to be able to hear them speak to us, we need to be able to see what it meant for them to try to love like this. To do this we must look at what their lives were like and how they understood themselves theologically.

In the first centuries of Christianity, before Constantine became emperor early in the fourth century, it was illegal to be a Christian. On the surface Christians were ordinary people who worked and had families, participated in everyday life with their neighbors, supported the government, and paid their taxes. They belonged to all classes in their society, and within the Roman Empire they came from many different peoples. They observed the proprieties of their society; they were not revolutionaries, and they did not directly threaten the social structures of their own times. With good reason early Christian writers like Justin Martyr[10] in the second century could claim that Christians were law abiding and peaceable just like their non-Christian neighbors.

Nevertheless Christians were not like other people. From the standpoint of their neighbors, they were "atheists." They did not acknowledge the existence of the gods who watched over the lives of individuals, cities, and empires with eyes quick to be angered by human disrespect. Christians recognized only one God, while they believed the gods of their pagan neighbors were merely demons masquerading as divinities. Early Christians therefore refused to participate in the kinds of pagan worship that the well-being of the Roman Empire was thought to depend upon. They would not even hold a variety of ordinary jobs that were touched by paganism: schoolteaching, acting, and metalworking, for example.[11]

Christians also stood out from the rest of their culture by their unusual love for each other in their communities. This love was neither abstract nor a simple matter of good feeling: it was a way of being together, a way of prayer, and a way of living in the world, rooted in their experience and understanding of the God who had come to them in the resurrected Jesus. This love manifested itself in their behavior to each other as well as in their prayer. Indeed

Christian love, Christian prayer, and Christian virtue were so in-
terwoven that the individual elements are hard for us to separate
in their early writings.[12] We will find that this same interconnection
of love, prayer, and virtue was passed on to the founders of monasticism.

As for their prayer, early Christians prayed both communally
and individually.[13] They prayed with the expectation that where
two or three were gathered, there the Holy Spirit would be with
them. They took individual prayer for granted as well. Regular
public daily services did not become commonplace until the fourth
century under the emperor Constantine. Nevertheless early Christians did not regard private prayer as being all that different from
communal prayer. Even when praying alone they knew they prayed
as part of the body of Christ. This meant that their private prayer,
rather than separating them from their brothers and sisters in
Christ, joined them all the closer. They prayed facing east, toward
the rising sun, at set times, between three and seven times a day.
Their prayer was partly spontaneous, partly based in Scripture—
the Psalms particularly, but the rest of the Old and New Testaments
as well—and it included intercessions and prayers for the world
as well as for the community and individuals.

Their prayer was joined to a serious discipline of life. In the
years before Constantine, being Christian was a risky business.
Although persecution was sporadic, Christians always knew that
they might have to give the ultimate witness to their faith through
martyrdom. For this reason, among others, early Christians insisted
on a backbone-stiffening discipline that seems mind-boggling to
us. Everyone agreed that sins committed before Baptism were forgiven. There was bitter debate in the second and third centuries,
however, about whether serious sin could be forgiven after Baptism.
Serious sin consisted of adultery, murder, and apostasy—that is,
caving in under often prolonged torture to renounce the faith, turn
over sacred books, or give away the whereabouts of other Christians.

When the emperor Constantine accepted Christianity in the
beginning of the fourth century, everything changed. Suddenly
Christianity was actually favored by the emperor. Churches were
built with public money, and public worship became the rule. There
were many new converts, and Christians prospered openly. To
some people, God had worked a miracle.[14]

At the same time other Christians were more ambiguous about the possibilities of living like their non-Christian neighbors. The blood of the martyrs had watered the church. Now there were no more martyrs, and the church began to have one of the major problems we struggle with in our own time: how to claim and live out fully what it means to be a Christian while trying to come to terms with a culture intent upon swallowing up Christian goals and values. Many people began asking whether it was possible to live a Christian life of love while being tied into the ordinary structures of society, owning property, holding a job, raising children, seeking social status, belonging to a family household. It is in this context that early monasticism arose, almost simultaneously in Greek- and Coptic-speaking Egypt, Palestine, and Syriac-speaking parts of the Roman Empire, and a little later in the Latin-speaking parts.

Contrary to what is often believed, this new monasticism in all its varieties did not consist of a small number of eccentric men and women living a similar life-style. Its many adherents were men and women of every kind of temperament from every social class and every part of the Roman Empire. The monastic movement of the fourth and fifth centuries embraced tightly structured large communities as well as informal ones, solitaries in the desert, and friends living together in single households.

We know about the beginnings of monasticism at the end of the third century, even before Constantine, from a surviving biography of Anthony, its first hero and teacher, written by a great fourth-century theologian and archbishop, Athanasius of Alexandria.[15] The story begins in a little town in the north of Egypt with an adolescent, orphaned, and well-off Anthony. He had been reared in a comfortable Christian home. A few months after his parents died he heard the story of the rich young ruler read in church from the Gospel of Matthew,[16] and in the story he heard Jesus say to him personally, "If you would be perfect, sell all you have and give to the poor and come, follow me." Anthony responded by giving away most of his property. A little while after, he disposed of the rest of it when he heard in that same church, "Take no thought for the morrow."

It was the phrase "If you would be perfect . . ." that had mobilized Anthony. To us the idea of perfection suggests legalism, rigidity, or perfectionism. To him and to those who followed him it was to be understood in terms of the Great Commandment, "You must love the Lord your God with all your heart, with all your soul, with all your strength, and with all your mind, and your neighbor as yourself."[17] Beginning on the edge of town and learning from the celibate men who already lived a special life of Christian discipline in the towns, Anthony finally moved out into the desert to begin the life of the first recorded Christian monk, at the same time founding an alternative Christian society. Not that he intended such a society originally: Anthony started as a hermit himself, but he soon found himself surrounded by disciples who wished to learn his way of life. He was sought out for advice by all sorts of people, including army officers, peasants, politicians, and other teachers like himself. Soon there were so many men and women in this new way of life that in the area around Anthony

> their cells in the hills were like tents filled with divine choirs—people chanting, studying, fasting, praying, rejoicing in the hope of future boons, working for the distribution of alms, and maintaining love and harmony among themselves. It was as if one truly looked on a land all its own—a land of devotion and righteousness. For neither perpetrator nor victim of injustice was there, nor complaint of a tax collector.[18]

By the time Anthony died at age 105 in the year 356, monastic communities were all over the Roman Empire, each with its own color but each also touched in a significant way by Egyptian monasticism.

Soon in the north of Egypt there were other little communities, each with its teacher, called the Abba (father)[19] or Amma (mother), and disciples, all of whom had renounced their personal property and family life, including marriage and status, in order to seek love and prayer. Among the male communities, each took its character from the particular discipline of the Abba. Some Abbas were mostly silent, preferring to teach by example, while others were outgoing, encouraging all who came near them with their love and their understanding of human frailty.

Shortly after Anthony, Pachomius, the other great founder of Egyptian monasticism, established more highly organized communities in the south. Nevertheless his goals were similar to Anthony's. According to his first Greek biography,[20] his initial encounter with Christians came after he had been conscripted into the army. As a cold, hungry, and miserable young soldier he was locked up with fellow conscripts in the city of Thebes. While he was there some Christians brought them food and other necessities, an act of charity that overwhelmed Pachomius. When he asked who they were, he was told that Christians are people

"who bear the name of Christ, the only Son of God, and they do all manner of good things for everyone, putting their hope on him who made the heaven and the earth and us [human beings]."[21]

Pachomius was so struck by this that he prayed to God, vowing that if he were allowed to escape, he would become a Christian. Later, after his release and seeking the will of God for himself, he heard his own call to the desert via the voice of an angel telling him three times,

"The Lord's will is to minister to the race of [human beings] in order to reconcile them to [Godself]."[22]

The communities Pachomius went on to establish were large, containing hundreds of men or women, and soon he was attracting so many people from so many parts of the world that he had to organize his dormitories according to the languages of their inhabitants.

In order to join Pachomius's communities, male and female monks had to give up property, family relationships,[23] and sexuality, taking up a discipline similar to those of northern Egypt: food, water, and sleep were regulated not to torture the body but in order to allow the monks as much freedom from the demands of the body as they could manage. Much of what they had to say about these demands and their effects upon us we can still recognize as true today when we admit our dependency upon well-prepared food and comfortable beds for our very sense of well-being, although we do not necessarily share their confidence in the usefulness of advice such as Arsenius gave:

"Abba Arsenius used to say that one hour's sleep is enough for a monk if he is a good fighter."[24]

Originally male monasticism was deliberately a lay movement. Seeking a way of living out the commands and promises of the gospel that gave freedom from the power games of everyday life in society, the monastic life for men represented a reversal of all ordinary social values. Egyptian monasticism's male founders believed that there was no way to exercise the authority of a priest at the same time one was trying to become free from the need to dominate and judge others.[25] The first Egyptian monastics, therefore, received the Eucharist at their local village churches from their parish priests. Not too far into the fourth century, however, it was deemed necessary for monastic communities to have their own priests. Within a short time bishops and archbishops were increasingly appointed from monastic ranks. Nevertheless ambiguity about exercising ecclesiastical power over others remained at least vestigially within the spirituality of early monasticism.

Women participated in monastic life as well, although it did not take precisely the same form or have the same meaning for women as it did for many men. Generally during this period most women did not have much control over their own lives and destinies. Outside of monasticism Christian women were always in significant ways at the disposal of husbands, fathers, or brothers. Women were expected to marry, and it is important to remember that for women a large portion of marriage was a matter of pregnancy, childbirth, and rearing children, all dangerous activities in those days.[26] For a man to take up the monastic life during this period could have very different meanings, according to his wealth and the status of his former life, whether, for example, he was of the senatorial rank as Arsenius was or a dirt-poor peasant accustomed to sleeping on the ground. For a woman it was, at the most basic level, to step into a realm of freedom from slavery to her body as well as freedom from the control of male relatives. At another level, as a monastic she was regarded as having put off "feminine weakness" and was allowed to mingle with and be taken seriously by her male colleagues in ways that were not possible for non-monastic women. For a woman to embrace the monastic life meant for her to claim emphatically Jesus' vision of a world in which a person's true identity came not from fulfilling society's role expectations but from living in the kingdom.

Female asceticism was extremely varied in its expression. Pachomius's sister started a monastery for women across the Nile at the same time as he founded his first monasteries for men.[27] Many women lived as consecrated virgins within their own family homes, while others lived together informally in Christian households in which they put into practice monastic ideals.[28] Some wealthy and aristocratic women chose to leave their family responsibilities, using their wealth and influence to found monasteries of their own for themselves and other women, to travel freely, and to find a place in the larger monastic world they shared with men.[29]

It is true that these monastic women as a group were being assimilated into a life-style that was still largely controlled and directed by men. But we must also remember that the new "life of virginity" gave individual women a freedom from male control and biological necessity, and that the monastic virtues shaping this new life were often in serious opposition to the dominant values with respect to women of the time.

All this being true, it is especially tragic that very little literature by monastic women exists from this early period that was considered worthy of being preserved (by the men who did the preserving!) compared with the many writings from male communities.

THE SHAPE OF EARLY MONASTIC PRAYER

When it comes to what the early monastic literature we will be using has to say about prayer, a first reading suggests that the monks said surprisingly little about it, directly. Considering that prayer is the one fundamental activity all the Abbas, Ammas, and disciples had in common, this can be baffling. Because they took prayer so much for granted as the fundamental activity of their lives, they may not have thought they needed to say much explicit about it, unless there was a special reason. More important, however, is that almost everything the Abbas and Ammas say has at least an indirect but significant bearing on prayer. This is because everything they did was rooted in prayer and was intended to foster prayer, as we will see in the later chapters of this book.

We can see this illustrated in the following saying of Abba Agathon:

> "A [person] who is angry, even if [that person] were to raise the dead, is not acceptable to God."[30]

Agathon intends his listeners to hear this as a warning that love is the basis of the whole spiritual life. If one is angry when one prays, whatever amazing spiritual feats that person might perform, he or she has seriously strayed from the way of the Christian life.

This does not mean that we do not pray when we are angry, because we are always to pray. It does mean that we must not believe we can separate our prayer from how we act toward other people; prayer and love of others are in many ways two sides of the same coin. Agathon's saying also warns us not to pray against anybody, not to be self-righteous, not to believe we are in a position to judge other people.

Monastic prayer was many faceted, and the dividing line between public and individual prayer was not as clear as we might expect it to be. The starting point of early monastic prayer, however, was common worship. This common worship was based first in the sacramental life of the church,[31] which they shared with non-monastics, and second in the regular prayer services of their own communities. The shared worship should remind us that perfect love of God and neighbor had its beginning and end in the gift of God to the world in Jesus Christ, in whose life and death we share. As we noted,[32] there were no priests in the first monastic communities. The first monks did not keep themselves separate from the rest of the church for their worship. They were dependent upon the local church for receiving the Lord's Supper, so that they were very often present for the Eucharist with the laity in worship. Later, because of practical considerations, male monks would be ordained for the purpose of serving their communities. It is important to remember that these monastic "churches" did not then thrive apart from the rest of the church but, indeed, functioned as a very important part of it.[33]

In the north of Egypt within the communities of male monastics, the men would gather on the weekends for common prayer based essentially in the Psalms and readings from other parts of Scripture. During the week they prayed by themselves, sometimes working and praying simultaneously—weaving baskets, making rope, or otherwise occupying their hands while leaving their minds free for meditation on Scripture or other forms of prayer. Sometimes they alternated prayer and work. Anthony followed the second pattern:

> When the holy Abba Anthony lived in the desert he was beset by [restless boredom], and attacked by many sinful thoughts. He said to God, "Lord, I want to be saved but these thoughts do not leave me alone; what shall I do in my affliction? How can I be saved?" A short while afterwards, when he got up to go out, Anthony saw a man like himself sitting at

his work, getting up from his work to pray, then sitting down and plaiting a rope, then getting up again to pray. It was an angel of the Lord sent to correct and reassure him. He heard the angel saying to him, "Do this and you will be saved." At these words, Anthony was filled with joy and courage. He did this, and he was saved.[34]

Notice that for his formal prayer, like the monastics who follow him, Anthony stands up and almost certainly prays with his arms outstretched in the form of the cross—a very old and very strenuous way to pray.

In the large male and female Pachomian communities in the south of Egypt, the practice arose of the community coming together to pray the Psalms at set times of the day and night. This pattern of daily prayer, which is called the monastic "office" or the "liturgy of the hours," became the dominant monastic practice in the rest of the Roman Empire. The early monastics in the north of Egypt did not approve of limiting prayer to fixed times, however, since they believed that such a pattern of prayer was an abandonment of a serious attempt to pray without ceasing.[35]

As for the individual prayer of the monks, there was clearly great variety in practice. Their literature portrays the monks as sometimes in intense conversation with God.[36] Occasionally we see them receiving visions or waking dreams.[37] Frequently we see them wrestling with various temptations and destructive states of mind so painful that one Abba described prayer as "warfare to the last breath."[38] For some, everyday prayer was largely nonverbal, but there was enormous difference even within this nonverbal prayer. As we will see in chapter 3, for example, Evagrius Ponticus taught a highly disciplined kind of "imageless prayer" or "pure prayer" that was very similar to Zen meditation.[39] The nearly nonverbal prayer of Macarius the Great, by contrast, was much more down to earth. It consisted simply of saying, in the face of temptation, "Lord, help!"[40]

To my knowledge, for all of them, however, the foundation of individual prayer consisted in the recitation from memory of the Psalms, just as communal prayer did. The Psalms were recited in order, 1 through 150, and then they would start over again. Some people were able to go through the whole Book of Psalms in twenty-four hours day after day, explaining Evagrius's remark:

"a great thing indeed—to pray without distraction; a greater thing still—to sing psalms without distraction."[41]

Meditation on other parts of Scripture made up a regular portion of all of their prayer.

THE EARLY LITERATURE ON PRAYER

Before we can go on to look more closely at what the early monastics have to teach us about our own prayer, it is necessary to know something about the surviving literature on prayer that we will draw on, and how we are to make sense of it.

First, there are collections of treatises, letters, and homilies that were either directly or indirectly influential on early monasticism itself. These works often contain details about early prayer and the theology that lay behind it that are not visible in a lot of the rest of the ancient material. Origen, the great third-century biblical scholar, left us a treatise on prayer,[42] for example, as well as many other texts that throw light on how the ancient monks were later to understand themselves and their goals.[43] Gregory of Nyssa, a Greek-speaking bishop of the fourth century who was deeply committed to the ideals and goals of monasticism, also left a commentary on the Lord's Prayer as well as other letters and essays on the goals of the Christian life and how we are to live it out. These, too, contribute to the kind of understanding of early monastic prayer necessary for our task.[44] Two more helpful essays were written by Evagrius Ponticus, a fourth-century teacher of the Egyptian desert who had a great deal of influence during his own time as well as on the later traditions of prayer in the whole church, east and west.[45] There are two more anonymous collections of texts that were enormously influential in the later church of the west, as well as in their own time. The first is the *Macarian Homilies*,[46] fifty sermons from a small monastic community probably in Syria. The second are the theological writings of Pseudo-Dionysius the Areopagite.[47]

Then there are the ancient biographies and stories of the monks. The *Life of Saint Anthony*, written by Athanasius, the fourth-century bishop and theologian of Alexandria, was an enormously influential work in its own time, and it still makes very good reading.[48] It is important to remember that we always meet an unnaturally heroic Anthony in this work because he is seen through the eyes of an archbishop rather than those of a monastic. Nevertheless in this biography we still are able not only to hear the fact of Anthony's life, but to experience something of the way the nonmonastic Christian culture saw and heard the early monastic teachers and their goals. Biographies of Pachomius have also survived, which are also a pleasure to read.[49]

One of the most interesting of these pieces of literature is Palladius's *Lausiac History*,[50] a collection of stories, some of which are true, some very obviously tall tales, about various monastic men and women of the first generations. This history includes a great deal of valuable information about the living arrangements of the monks as well as records of conversations between Palladius and the monks he visited, such as the famous Didymus the Blind.

Another fascinating collection, *The History of the Monks of Syria*, was written by the fifth-century bishop Theodoret of Cyrrhus. This work not only records what he knew about the beginnings of monasticism around the city of Antioch, it also includes accounts of monks he actually knew. One of the nicest stories is about his visits as a child with his mother to Peter the Galatian in which Peter's servant would try to recruit Theodoret to the monastic life, while, as Theodoret tells us,

> that inspired man did not agree that this [should] happen, adducing in argument the love my parents had for me. He often sat me on his knees and fed me with grapes and bread.[51]

In many places in Theodoret's history we are also given intimate glimpses of Theodoret's mother as she interacted with the monks. This is particularly valuable in light of the scarcity of this kind of material concerning women.[52]

An enormously influential Western writer who spent some time with the monastics of Egypt and wrote an account of his conversations with them is John Cassian. He, particularly, has a lot to tell us about prayer, not only in the Egyptian desert but also in his own sixth-century Italian monastery.[53]

The most wonderful of the early monastic literature, however, are the collections of *Sayings of the Desert Fathers*,[54] and it is this material that really provides the center for our discussion of love and prayer in this book. These texts consist of short sayings and stories of the the great teachers that circulated and were then collected, presumably, for the instruction of later disciples and Abbas. This literature, although hard to read because of its ambiguity and seeming lack of consistency, often gives us such an intimate picture of the desert teachers and their students that we feel ourselves there with them. When a disciple asks for advice with "Give me a word, Abba," we hear the response directed to ourselves in the present as much as it was to the ancient disciple.

At first glance many of the sayings seem to be almost in a kind of shorthand, so that they appear to make almost no sense at all. In many cases I suspect that the Ammas and Abbas only had to say a few words to their listeners, who would know just what they meant without the teacher having to elaborate. After all, they lived close together, and the disciples were accustomed to revealing all their thoughts to their teachers. We see this kind of verbal brevity in a saying attributed to Abba Ammonas, a disciple of Anthony and later a bishop:

> Abba Ammonas said, "I have spent fourteen years in Scetis asking God night and day to grant me the victory over anger."[55]

What does this saying mean, and what was its occasion? On the surface Ammonas has clearly said that he has a problem with anger, but why should such a saying be remembered? The context of the monastic struggle with the passions provides the clue.[56] The chances are that Ammonas had been asked for help by a disciple struggling against his own anger who was probably discouraged by the small amount of progress he was making. This was Ammonas's reply, and its meaning would have been clear to his listeners. They would have understood it as encouragement as they struggled with their own anger or anything else in themselves with which they persistently struggled, for discouragement over the slowness of Christian growth was a major problem for disciples then as it is for us today. So the disciple heard, "If the abba is still struggling after all these years, why should I be discouraged? This is no more than I should expect in the life I have chosen." The first rule for reading this material, then, is to remember that almost all of it has more layers of meaning than would appear on the surface.

Sometimes this literature is hard to read because the teachers believed that people often learn better if they are allowed to work things out for themselves, rather than being hit over the head with direct advice. For this reason many of the sayings employ what I call the indirect method of teaching. With this method a disciple asks a question or does something that the teacher replies to by giving an answer whose meaning the disciple must unravel. Here is an example:

> A brother asked Abba Sisoes: "I long to guard my heart." The old man said to him: "And how can we guard the heart if our tongue leaves the door of the fortress open?"[57]

By asking about guarding the heart, the disciple wants the Abba to tell him how he can keep God in his thoughts at all times, but the teacher does not tell him directly. "The tongue" in this literature refers to talking. The teacher, therefore, turns the question upside down, letting the disciple work out his reference to the tongue as a gentle reminder that his problem is not how to remember God in his heart but rather how to control his conversation, so as not to gossip, show off how much he knows or how holy he is, or waste time.

As I said at the beginning of this chapter, prayer is a shared life with God. For the Abbas and Ammas prayer is so important that one of them simply equates it with the kingdom of heaven.[58] For them prayer is the pearl of great price, the treasure found in a field, for which we sell everything else. Yet the monastic teachers find no gap between the world of prayer and the ordinary life we lead. There is no "holy" life that calls us to renounce parts of ourselves as unworthy. If we are to pray, we are to love, and for both love and prayer all of ourselves with nothing left out is needed. It is not easy to learn to bring all of ourselves to this adventure of prayer and love. Fortunately we do not have to learn by ourselves. We have not only the prayers of our ancient Christian ancestors to support us but their teaching as well to give us guidance and insight. So we turn with them to begin this adventure by exploring the world of love God created us for and reflecting on our ways of living in it.

Chapter 2

Living into the Image of God

*T*hat our wholeness as human beings depends upon living out the Great Commandment is the most fundamental of all early monastic convictions. The starting point of a life of prayer is to know, no matter how dimly, that we are created for and called to love: "You shall love the Lord your God with all your heart, and all your strength, and all your mind, and your neighbor as yourself."[1] Love is the final goal of the life of prayer, and loving and learning how to love are the daily work and pleasure of prayer. In approaching this goal with the help of our ancestors in the faith, we need to consider their understanding of how the image of God binds us all together in love; how sin and the passions distort the image and make love difficult or impossible; and how the virtues, cultivated in a life of prayer, make it possible to overcome temptation and be reconciled with God, our neighbor, and ourselves.

GOD'S LOVE FOR US AND THE PERSISTENCE OF THE IMAGE

The early church believed that God's love for us as human beings precedes, enables, and gives meaning to all human love and prayer. This love of God for us goes back to our very creation. God brought—and now brings—human beings into existence as images of God's own self simply because of God's love. The importance the monastics placed on God's love for us can hardly be over-stressed.

As images of God, we are beloved by God, who loves us as unwaveringly and responsively as a mother loves her baby. Macarius describes the emotional tone of God's love in this way:

> A baby, even though it is powerless to accomplish anything or with its own feet to go to its mother, still it rolls and makes noises and cries as it seeks its mother. . . . And she picks it up and fondles it and feeds it with great love. This is also what God, the Lover of [humankind], does to the person that comes to [God] and ardently desires [God].[2]

God's love is not the love of a dispassionate and just king for his distant subjects. It is intimate, tender, and vulnerable, as a mother's is for her baby.

Sin does not destroy God's love and yearning for us. Sometimes it is said that the real wonder of our faith is that God loves us in spite of our unlovableness. Our monastic ancestors would find such a way of speaking quite alien. To God we are lovable and valuable, however damaged we may be, as this quotation from the *Sayings* makes very clear:

> A soldier asked Abba Mius if God accepted repentance. After the old man had taught him many things he said, "Tell me, my dear, if your cloak is torn, do you throw it away?" He replied, "No, I mend it and use it again." The old man said to him, "If you are so careful about your cloak, will not God be equally careful about [God's] creature?"[3]

God's love is always there whether or not we can feel it, whether we seem good or bad to ourselves or to others, or whether or not we respond to God. It is a love that does not depend upon our "being good." That this is true has enormous consequences for what we need to be able to pray, as we will see in the next chapter.

Nor does sin destroy completely our ability to respond to God's love for us. Out of the tender and persistent love God has for us, each of us has been given God's own image that can never be completely lost. According to our Christian ancestors, although human life as we know it without God may appear hopelessly broken, God's image remains within us—partially erased or covered over but still there.[4] This means that, however skewed our vision

of God, others, and ourselves becomes, something in us still rec-
ognizes God. The image of God that is in us is the part of ourselves
that never stops desiring to move toward love.

Even if there seems to be no room for human freedom at all,
that part of ourselves is still always able to choose to cry out for
help to make the tiniest movement toward love. In the words of
the *Macarian Homilies*,

> Just as [the woman with the issue of blood] . . . could not be cured,
> nevertheless, she had feet by which she could hasten to the Lord, and
> approaching him, she obtained a cure. . . ; so also a person, even though
> he is heavily afflicted by evil passions and is blinded by the darkness
> of sin, nevertheless, he possesses the ability to will to cry out and beg
> Jesus that he come and bring eternal salvation to his soul.[5]

This means that no matter how thoughtless or even depraved a
person may seem to be, because of the persistent presence of the
image of God, there is a fundamental goodness in every human
being that always connects us to God and to each other as well.

This is not to say that these ancient teachers of love were
ignorant of the existence of evil in the world. Once,

> Abraham, the disciple of Abba Agathon, questioned Abba Poemen say-
> ing, "How do the demons fight against me?" Abba Poemen said to him,
> "The demons fight against you? They do not fight against us at all as
> long as we are doing our own will. For our own wills become the demons,
> and it is these which attack us in order that we may fulfill them. But if
> you want to see who the demons really fight against, it is against Moses
> and those who are like him."[6]

The monastics warned against blaming our behavior or our situation
on something outside ourselves when we, in fact, are responsible.
Yet they did not psychologize evil as merely a projection of our
own desires and therefore traceable only to personal acts. By their
language of Satan and the demons they mean to acknowledge the
reality and pervasiveness of malice in the world. Although people
often hurt one another without intending to, people also genuinely
intend to hurt each other.

In this light it is especially important to notice that their belief
in the persistence and durability of the image of God goes against
one of the most painful and widespread modern Christian convictions, that in the sight of the good and holy God human beings
are all lower than worms, contaminated by the filthiness of sin.

Such a conviction encourages us to think and feel that although we have an assurance of God's love for us displayed in Christ, we should never approach God without an awareness of our sinfulness and unworthiness.

The best theology of the early church emphatically rejects such self-hatred. In fact in one of his letters to the monks, Anthony says:

"[The one] who can love himself [or herself], loves all."[7]

Conversely, an attitude of self-contempt or self-hatred is horribly destructive of our ability to love and to pray. It fosters judgmentalism, envy, rage, masochism, and manipulative relationships, to name only a few of its more overt problems. It also encourages us from an early age to hide our real feelings and motivations from ourselves as well as others and therefore necessarily also from God. Growth in love, however, requires that we be able to recognize our own anger or pleasure or anxiety in any relationship, whether with God, a spouse, a friend, or coworker, much less, as the gospel stresses, with a stranger or even an enemy. The need to recognize our deep feelings and motivations if we are to grow in love is the reason the early monastic literature stresses self-knowledge.

LOVE AND OUR KINSHIP WITH OTHERS

That we are all made in the image of God meant that as we are intimately related to God, we are also related intimately to each other. Abba Anthony used to say,

"From our neighbour are life and death. If we do good to our neighbour, we do good to God: if we cause our neighbour to stumble, we sin against Christ."[8]

Because of the presence of the image of God within us, what affects the welfare of one of us affects us all, God included.

The bonds that connect us are the bonds of love, God's love for us, which draws us, but also our love for God and neighbor, which can never be separated from each other. Remember Dorotheos of Gaza's illustration of this reality to which I referred in chapter 1.[9] Imagine, he asks, that we have drawn a circle with a compass. God is at the center, where the point of the compass went. Now imagine that the outside of the circle is the world, and the lives of human beings are represented by many straight lines drawn from the outside to the center. Notice how as you follow a single line from the outside toward God, all the lines come closer together. This is the way human beings relate to God and to each other, for

> the closer they are to God, the closer they become to one another; and the closer they are to one another, the closer they become to God.

The diagram works in reverse as well. If you follow a single line from the center out to the edge again, you notice that all the lines become farther apart as they go away from the center. This, Dorotheos says, is because

> this is the very nature of love. The more we are turned away from and do not love God, the greater the distance that separates us from our neighbor. If we were to love God more, we should be closer to God, and through love of [God] we should be more united in love to our neighbor; and the more we are united to our neighbor the more we are united to God.

We cannot love God and hate or even be indifferent to our neighbor. Growth in the love of God also has to include love of those images of God with whom we share our world.

This love of other people who are God's images is not an abstract love of humanity, a warm feeling of kinship toward humankind in general. It is very easy to love in the abstract—the homeless, children, the suffering. It is not so hard to love those with whom we have infrequent or only surface contact when love is defined as a kind of unfocused friendly feeling.

There was nothing abstract or unfocused about the love of which Dorotheos is speaking. Love of neighbor included taking very seriously the actual day-to-day welfare of the real people with whom the monks came into contact. There is a whole series of spectacular stories in the *Sayings* about the extravagant and very particular love individual monks displayed in difficult situations toward unlikely recipients of their care. A monk goes through an elaborate deception to win a prostitute away from prostitution.[10] Another monk supports an alcoholic he has met in the market for years on his tiny earnings.[11] A bishop endows an unmarried and pregnant girl with expensive bed sheets when the self-righteous Christians around her abandon her because of her sin.[12]

What the monastics sought for themselves, however, was more than the ability to love spectacularly. What they wanted was to be able to love the ordinary people around them as images of God on an everyday basis. They knew that love required them to be attentive to the people with whom they spent most of their time, people whom they could find irritating from such close contact, or people whose presence they might so much take for granted that they hardly noticed them at all. It would appear that for them, as for us, it was easy to love in a crisis situation. When it came to the "little things" of ordinary life, however, it was another matter. That is why Abba Poemen gave this advice about love:

> "There is nothing greater in love than that a [person] lay down [that person's] life for his [or her] neighbor. When a [person] hears a complaining word and struggles against himself [or herself] and does not . . . begin to complain; when a [person] bears an injury with patience, and does not look for revenge; that is when a [person] lays down his [or her] life for his [or her] neighbor."[13]

It is often said that if we really love each other, the little things do not matter. The monastic teachers knew that such a disregard for these little things is more often than not experienced by the people around us as a contemptuous or at least thoughtless disregard of their everyday welfare.

So far we have spoken as though the bonds that connect us to each other through the image of God are always individual. In our own period, especially since the eighteenth century, we are accustomed to stressing our individuality and our uniqueness. Like snowflakes, we know that each of us is different from all the rest. We value and work hard for our separateness and our freedom to be who we are. Certainly the story of the image of God supports us in our enjoyment of our individuality. Our ancestors fought hard to affirm that God appeared among us as a real, individual, flesh-and-blood human being who was born, lived, and died in a real, particular time and place. The story of the image of God tells us that it is good that we are all unique human beings and that we should value each other accordingly as individuals.

What we have almost lost in our modern world, however, is our heart knowledge of the strength of the bonds that unite us in a common humanity in a shared physical world. The story of the creation of Adam and Eve, their fall, and the coming of God in the incarnation for their healing is an account of each Christian life, but it is also the story of the whole human race. In a profound way our ancestors knew that although it does not seem to be the case, as human beings our unity is as significant as our individuality.

Such an understanding has real significance for helping us make sense of our human situation. In our emphasis on being individuals we forget that we live in a whole world thoroughly damaged by sin. And this sin is not just the sum total of individual choices for evil across the generations. It has a life of its own that is self-perpetuating in human society, often seemingly quite independent of the good intentions of individual members of that society. This collective human sin encourages, supports, and perpetuates our separation from each other into groups of "them and us." It operates in nations, classes, professions, races, sexes, neighborhoods, friendships, families, churches, and groups within churches, who reinforce our feeling of belonging to them by encouraging our estrangement from outsiders about whose well-being we could not possibly be concerned. It is at work, too, in our estrangement from our earth when we regard it as simply there to be exploited.

SIN AND THE PASSIONS

The early monastic teachers were well aware that we live in a world that is thoroughly and systematically damaged by sin. Although they used the language of sin to speak of this damage, however, much more frequently they spoke of "the passions."[14] In this way ancient Christian writers used the popular psychology of their day to describe a major portion of the internal human dynamics that keep all human beings from functioning as God intends us to function. Although it is not a familiar psychology to us, their concept of the passions can be enormously helpful to the modern Christian who would learn to love better. Surprisingly little in their ancient perspective is at odds in a serious way with much modern psychological theory.[15]

The passions, as these teachers spoke of them, afflict all human beings as a result of living in a fallen world. The origins of individual sin, the passions are habits of seeing, feeling, thinking, and acting that characteristically blind us to who we ourselves, our neighbors, and God really are so that we are not able to respond appropriately, rationally, and lovingly. The passions distort everything.

What are some examples of the passions? Envy that makes it impossible to see a neighbor except through the lense of resentment is a passion. The kind of smoldering irritability toward a family member that results in continual touchiness about everything the other person does or says is a passion. Anorexia nervosa, an obsession about body size that tells its sufferer that she is fat when she is actually starving is a passion. Sexual desire that takes no interest in its object as a human being is a passion, as is depression, which makes all of life look hopeless. A desire to gossip; perfectionism; a need to be in control all the time; a habitual distrust of other people's motives; a constant need for approval; fear of silence or being alone; obsessive cravings—all are passions.

Evagrius Ponticus, a monastic teacher of the fourth century, compiled an apparently systematic list of eight passions: gluttony, lust "for bodies," avarice, depression, anger, restless boredom, love of praise, and pride.[16] This list is not as systematic as it appears, however, for each of these passions represents not so much specific behavior as whole overlapping ways of relating to the world, ourselves, and other people. Gluttony, for example, is far less a desire to overeat as it is a desire for variety in life that leads us never to be able to be satisfied with what we have.[17] This in turn leads to a kind of acquisitiveness that makes us confuse what we own with who we are. Out of such a confusion grows fear of losing what we have to others, the need to dominate others, and a boredom that can be satisfied only by feeding our hunger to possess goods or other people or power.

The monastic teachers are not using the term *passion* in the same way modern English does. English uses *passion* to describe a whole range of strong emotions, without distinguishing between negative or positive. We use the same word to speak of a passion for the poor, sexual passion, a passion for chocolates, or terrible anger. The early monastics use *passion* as a negative term only. If a habit of mind, a way of seeing, feeling, or acting does not keep us from seeing and responding to God, other people, and ourselves as they really are, the monastics would not call it a passion. For the monastics no state of mind or desire, no matter how strong, qualifies as a passion unless it is destructive of love. It is important to know that they absolutely did not identify positive emotions and desires like love, compassion, or courage as passions.

It is even more important to notice that with the notion of passions the ancient church is offering modern Christians an alternative model for understanding reality. Steeped as we are in eighteenth-century Enlightenment ways of understanding, we tend to make a fundamental opposition between "feeling" and "reasoning." To look at a situation rationally means to look at it logically, without the "muddying" presence of emotions, such as pity, affection, or the desire to protect the vulnerable. Emotion, we have been told, is subjective, personal, and private, and it keeps us from the truth. Emotion always takes individual circumstances into account. Reason or logic, by contrast, is objective, impersonal, and publically verifiable. In popular thought science depends upon the use of reason and the exclusion of emotion, which is its enemy.[18]

Our ancestors would have found such a division between rationality and emotion baffling, especially for Christians. For them it is a fundamental theological conviction that reality itself is grounded in God, whose basic being is love. To be made in the image of God means that we cannot see anyone or anything else as it truly is without seeing as God sees, that is, through the lense of love. They were convinced that rather than a commitment to the truth excluding love, only the presence of real love could be the basis of seeing the truth at all. Love and rationality, therefore, rather than being enemies of each other, must be all of a piece. Reasoning about another person, about God, and about ourselves is only reliable when it is grounded in love. Moreover, really loving depends upon our ability to see and know another person, God, and even ourselves as more than an extension of our own needs, desires, or fantasies.

If the passions prevent love as they obscure our ability to see reality as it is, they also increasingly take away our freedom to make real choices and act on them. What we cannot clearly see, we cannot make genuine decisions about, and this affects every aspect of our lives. This is equally the case whether we are in the grip of our own short-term bad mood, such as irritability or boredom, or our longer-term habits and states of mind. Perfectionism, which will come up in more than one place in the following pages, is one of the most difficult passions that we share with our monastic forebears. The fear of abandonment and the need for approval that many of us have carried over from childhood also take away adult freedom to a lesser or greater degree.

Are the passions the same as sin? Are we responsible for them or not? It is probably true for most people that we never consciously chose to be subject to our most destructive passions, yet we also assent to the presence of those passions within us. Take the example of a person who spends money compulsively. On the one hand, modern American society constantly encourages unnecessary consumption. On the other, no one forces a person to spend money on luxuries. Likewise, a person who was battered as a child very frequently becomes a battering parent. The pattern of battering is inherited, yet it is also chosen. It is this baffling double origin of the passions that leads much of the monastic literature to use the language of demons to speak of the ambiguous source and power of the passions. They are experienced as hostile and exterior to us in some ways, yet the passions do not ultimately have power over us without our assent.

This is easy to see in the case of anger, which Evagrius speaks of as "the most fierce passion."[19] He describes it as

> a boiling and stirring up of wrath against one who has given injury—or is thought to have done so. It constantly irritates the soul and above all at the time of prayer it seizes the mind and flashes the picture of the offensive person before one's eyes.

Note that anger is here described as resulting from a real or imagined injury, and thus the angry person is not responsible for the origins of his anger. Nevertheless the angry person can choose to nurse that anger to the point where he is entirely given over to it, for "both anger and hatred increase anger,"[20] or he can fight against it and refuse to let it reach the point of becoming destructive. The child of alcoholic parents did not choose her parents or the passion of insecurity that plagues the adult she becomes. Yet as an adult she is not simply a victim: an adult can either fight against that insecurity or choose to let it blossom into destructive jealousy, rage, hopelessness, or cynicism.

The early monastics were not, finally, all that interested in whether we are responsible for the origins of the passions that bind us. The passions are wounds[21] within us that destroy our lives and the lives of others around us. Our job, they were convinced, is to fight against the passions and seek healing with the help of God and each other in order to be able to love as we were made to love. This is why so many of the ancient monastics spent so much of their time in and out of prayer wrestling with their passions, and why I will often speak of the passions and their healing in the following pages.

THE VIRTUES

The presence of the image of God within the Christian makes Christian prayer possible. This image out of which we pray is what ties human beings to God as well as to each other. According to our foremothers and forefathers, however, the image and likeness of God does not manifest itself simply as a warm feeling of relationship to God and other people. At root our kinship with God is a kind of character originally stamped on our very being by God's intention for us, a pattern of seeing, understanding, feeling, and acting toward God, ourselves, and others. The early monastics often speak of the pattern of this character in terms of "the virtues."

These monastics believed that in ordinary life as we know it, however, the image of God in each of us—that original character or pattern of the virtues God intends for us—has been and continues to be seriously damaged by sin and the passions. Sin and the passions take away our ability to see and understand our relationships with God, ourselves, and one another. Instead we find ourselves swallowed up by distorted habits, feelings, and attitudes about possessions, status, work, security, guilt, sex, love, family, and friends. Because our prayer is part of who we are, our prayer shares in this damage.

The message of the early church, however, is that God does not abandon us in our damaged condition. An essential element in the work of Christ is the healing of the wounded image of God. For the monastics, as well as for their nonmonastic counterparts in the early church, this healing is not a magical occurrence that takes place all at once but rather is gradual. Ongoing healing continues as the Christian character that the virtues constitute is developed, and sin, the passions, and their effects are weakened or replaced. Prayer is never separate from this process.

How did the early monastics understand the virtues? New monks in the desert of Egypt in the fourth century often made the same mistake many modern Christians make: they wanted the Christian virtues to be a list of rules that would always tell them what to do and even feel. The Abbas and Ammas insisted, however, that the Christian life is not a matter of following rules or even keeping ascetic disciplines. The development of the virtues is the development of love. One of the *Sayings* states this emphatically and humorously.

A brother asked an old man: "there are two monks: one stays quietly in his cell, fasting for six days at a time, and laying many austerities upon himself: and the other ministers to the sick. Which of them is more acceptable to God?" The old man answered: "If the brother, who fasts six days, even hung himself up by his nostrils, he could never be the equal of him who ministers to the sick."[22]

For the great Ammas and Abbas, practicing the virtues was never a matter of making lists of rules of behavior monks ought to follow and then following the list rigidly.

The Christian virtues lie much deeper than this. The virtues are Christian patterns of seeing, feeling, and understanding as well as acting that affect everything we do and everything we are. They are the internal laws that make us who we are, as Christians, but also as human beings. As the metaphor of Dorotheos's circle, and how within it human beings are related to each other and God would suggest, the virtues have to do always with love of God and of neighbor. In the words of one Abba,

"Virtue . . . leads to God and unites us with one another."[23]

The monastic disciplines of fasting, lack of property, control of sleep and sexuality, silence, and sometimes even prayer itself are valuable only insofar as they help to form and promote the virtues, which enable love. In this sense the development of the virtues, like prayer itself, is never truly private: it is for the upbuilding of the community rather than simply personal fulfillment. As Abba Poemen recalled:

Abba Theonas said, "Even if [people] acquire virtue, God does not grant [them] grace for [themselves] alone." He knew that he was not faithful in his own labor, but that if he went to his companion, God would be with him.[24]

Although they are far from constituting the whole of the image and likeness of God within us, the virtues are a fundamental part of it. Dorotheos says,

Truly when God made [human beings, God] sowed the virtues in [them], as it says: "Let us make [human beings] to our own image and likeness." To [God's] image, since God made the soul incorruptible and self-determining; [God's] likeness, which means having similar virtues. Does the scripture not say: "Be merciful, as your heavenly Father is merciful"? And: "Be holy, for I am holy"? And again, the Apostle says: "Be kind to one another!" In the Psalm: "The Lord is kind to those who are waiting for [God]." There are more like these all showing this likeness to God.[25]

The virtues make us like God in the most intimate manner possible, by allowing us to share in God's mercy through our own exercise of mercy and, similarly, in God's holiness and kindness as well as in other divine characteristics that God has placed in us as part of what it means to be human.

Even if it is easy to see all our sin and brokenness and hard to see any of the virtues in ourselves, the virtues are never really beyond recovery. This is because they are natural to us in a way sin can never be. Dorotheos adds to what he has already said about the image and likeness of God, "God gave us the virtues as an endowment of our nature, but [God] did not endow us with vices."[26] This is a far cry from the modern conviction that sin, self-centeredness, and disregard for the welfare of the neighbor are somehow natural to human beings while compassion, forgiveness, and even wholeness are not!

Natural or not, however, this does not mean that the Abbas and Ammas believed that Christians receive the virtues as a gift along with Baptism or simply through asking for them in prayer. The virtues are surely a gift of God in a fundamental sense: one cannot simply will oneself to love God, other people, or even oneself. Without that gift the prospect is hopeless. The monastic teachers believed at the same time, however, that none of this happens without human effort. We must cultivate behavior appropriate to the virtues within us over a long period.

Perhaps even more fundamental to the development of the virtues than cultivating behavior appropriate to them was the monk's conscious choice of them.

Abba Anthony said, "Whoever hammers a lump of iron, first decides what he is going to make of it, a scythe, a sword, or an axe. Even so we ought to make up our minds what kind of virtue we want to forge or we labor in vain."[27]

The ancient Christian, no more than we, could not hope for growth in love or prayer without thinking, praying through, and deciding what human qualities she or he really wants to grow into. What does it mean to a Christian to have independence and self-reliance? Forgiveness? A sense of honor? Humility? Patience? Being identified as a person "above reproach"? An ability to work consensually with others? Hospitality? Quiet? Not all of these "virtues" may really be Christian, however ancient or modern culture values them. With the conflicting values of both ancient and modern life pulling us in many directions, often in subtly anti-Christian ones, no one could or can afford simply to try to be a good Christian and hope for the best without making real choices.

Just as important as making decisions about which virtues are truly "Christian," however, is being able to make a realistic assessment about which virtues we are temperamentally able and willing to develop. The monastic teachers were convinced that we are very different from one another, and the real healing of our ability to love requires us to take this into account in a very serious way. A brother once asked his Abba for advice on what kind of work he ought to do—by which he was really asking about what virtues he needed to develop. His Abba told him this:

> God knows what is good. I have heard it said that one of the Fathers asked Abba Nisterus the Great, the friend of Abba Anthony, and said to him, "What good work is there that I could do?" He said to him, "Are not all actions equal? Scripture says that Abraham was hospitable and God was with him. David was humble, and God was with him. Elias loved interior peace and God was with him. So, do whatever you see your soul desires according to God and guard your heart."[28]

In the selection of the virtues, most of us would be much happier and less burdened by unnecessary guilt if we could learn with the early monastics to be much more realistic about evaluating the limitations and advantages of our own temperaments as well as the temperaments of those around us.

TEMPTATION

Now that we have talked about the way early monastic teachers spoke of the relationship between love, sin, and the passions and the virtues, we must turn to one more major topic the Abbas and

Ammas consistently addressed as crucial to the development of love: temptation. Most of us do not quite know how to think about it. Temptation is not sin; put in the form of a proposition, we know this and believe it. Finding ourselves having to struggle against it is another matter. We respond by great attacks of guilt that demoralize us, making temptation all that harder to deal with.

Temptation may seem to us to be very close to sin in some of the more conspicuous forms it takes. This is true, for example, when it comes as the urge to indulge the passion of anger by telling another person who has been giving us a hard time exactly what we think of him. It seems equally close as we feel the urge to give in to another person's bullying, knowing as we do that on a long-term basis bullying and our passivity in response to it hurts both us and the other person. To a married person struggling with the desire to become sexually involved with someone who is not his or her spouse, the line between sin and temptation may appear to be almost invisible.

The Abbas and Ammas did not believe that temptation is sin, and they expended a lot of energy trying to help the brothers and sisters understand its inevitability.

> A brother came to see Abba Poemen and said to him, "Abba, I have many thoughts and they put me in danger." The old man led him outside and said to him, "Expand your chest and do not breathe in." He said, "I cannot do that." Then the old man said to him, "If you cannot do that, no more can you prevent thoughts from arising, but you can resist them."[29]

Temptation is as natural and generally as morally neutral as breathing. A human being cannot hold her breath forever; we cannot help but suffer temptation.

Furthermore, they were convinced that failure to be tempted in any way is no sign of holiness. Evagrius Ponticus, for example, suggests that God does not allow a really weak person to be tempted, because her or his falling into sin is so likely. Other Abbas simply state that some people have no temptations because they give in to them at the very moment they arise. Abba Cyrus of Alexandria put it this way when asked about sexual sin:

> "If you do not think about it, you have no hope, for if you are not thinking about it, you are doing it. I mean, [the one] who does not fight

against the sin and resist it in his [or her] spirit will commit the sin physically."[30]

In fact our ancestors knew that our growth and even our very life as human beings depend upon our ongoing fight with real temptations.

"Take away temptations and no-one will be saved,"

says Evagrius Ponticus.[31] Why is this? First, remember that one of the more prominent features of our passions is that they are often invisible or nearly invisible to us. It is by observing even the temptations that we give in to that we are able to recognize and thus fight against the true nature of our deep passions. Origen in the third century said in his treatise "On Prayer,"

> What our soul has received is unknown to all save God—is unknown even to ourselves; but it is manifested by means of temptations; so that it may be no longer unknown what kind of persons we are, but rather that we should also know ourselves and be aware, if we will, of our own faults and give thanks for the good results manifested to us of temptations.[32]

Here is a nice example from the *Sayings* of the way a temptation revealed one monk's passions to him, so that he could deal with them. The temptations, which he gave in to, were to surrender to his irritability and to move away from other people.

> A brother was restless in the community and often moved to anger. So he said: "I will go, and live somewhere by myself. And since I shall be able to talk or listen to no one, I shall be tranquil, and my passionate anger will cease." He went out and lived alone in a cave. But one day he filled his jug with water and put it on the ground. It happened suddenly to fall over. He filled it again, and again it fell. And this happened a third time. And in a rage he snatched up the jug and broke it. Returning to his right mind, he knew that the demon of anger had mocked him, and he said: . . . "I will return to the community. Wherever you live, you need effort and patience and above all God's help."[33]

The brother in the story at first believed that his angry outbursts were caused by his living so close to other people. Only after he gave in to the urge to cut himself off from the community did he learn that his real problem was a combination of ongoing anger in himself, lack of effort and patience, and a need for God's grace. Presumably struggling and thinking through further temptations to anger will help him get a deeper hold on the nature of that anger.

The other significant way that we are dependent on temptation for our growth in the Christian life has to do with compassion. The monks were convinced that where we cannot feel compassion toward other people struggling with the passions, sin, or temptation, we cannot love. Once a priest was annoyed by a group of monks who were not behaving themselves, and so he went to their worship service and took their monastic garments away from them.

> Afterwards, his heart was moved, he repented and went to see Abba Poemen, obsessed by his thoughts. He brought the monastic habits of the brothers and told him all about it. The old man said to him, "Don't you sometimes have something of the old Adam in you?" The priest said, "I have my share of the old Adam." The abba said to him, "Look, you are just like the brethren yourself; if you have even a little share of the old Adam, then you are subject to sin in the same way." So the priest went and called the brothers and asked their pardon; and he clothed them in the monastic habit again and let them go.[34]

If the goal of the Christian life is love, without compassion we miss the goal altogether. What gives us compassion is knowing something firsthand about the pain another person is suffering or has suffered in her or his struggle with temptation, even if the struggle is lost. In our life in God, nothing is ever wasted. Even our own worst falls from temptation into sin can serve us well as they equip us to love the one who, like us, has also sinned, whether this person be neighbor, spouse, or stranger.

One word of caution: We must take the relationship between the temptations and the passions seriously enough that we recognize that sometimes what we think of as one kind of temptation is actually the sign of a more serious passion that must be addressed. To use a clear example: You consistently can hardly make yourself get out of bed in the morning to go to work. Taken at face value, you might want to believe that you are being tempted daily to give in to the passion of laziness to stay home in bed. The truth, however, may very well be something quite different. You may have a soul-crushing job that you are afraid to quit because you fear looking for another one; in this case your passion has to do with fear of new experiences or fear of financial disaster or whatever. Or you may be exhausted because you are not going to bed early enough. Or you may not be able to face the combination of work and home responsibilities because there are too many of them for one person to manage.

Our prayer about our temptations, then, like our prayer in which we wrestle with the passions, may need to include some real struggles to understand the origins of our temptations. Some of this kind of prayer can be very painful as we recognize things in ourselves we may not have wanted to see.

In other, simpler cases, however, the Abbas give other advice:

> Abba Macarius was asked, "How should one pray?" The old man said, "There is no need at all to make long discourses; it is enough to stretch out one's hands and say, 'Lord, as you will, and as you know, have mercy.' And if the conflict grows fiercer say, 'Lord, help!' [God] knows very well what we need and [God] shews us [God's] mercy."[35]

RECONCILIATION, HEALING, AND HOPE

Thus the story of the image of God and the recovery of love as the monastics told it is not so much about sin as it is about healing. It is a story whose very depths are hope. To live and pray out of that story is to learn as surely as it is possible to learn anything that estrangement from ourselves, one another, the physical world, and God is neither natural nor permanent. The promise of the story is this: In God all things are finally healed. Some of that healing will only be completed in ways we cannot know in the final renewal of all things in God. But much more than most of us are ever willing to imagine can be healed in the course of this life as well if we truly seek it and do not dictate to God what shape that healing is to take. I believe that in this process of healing, in the reconciling mercy of God, nothing that has happened to us or anything that we have been or done will ever finally be lost or wasted.

The healing promised to us is also the healing of all the relationships of all God's people. In the words of Anthony, Jesus has gathered us, is gathering us, and he will continue to gather

> us out of all regions, till he should make resurrection of our hearts from the earth, and teach us that we are all of one substance, and members of one another. For [the one] who loves his [or her] neighbor, loves God: and [the one who] loves God, loves his [or her] own soul.[36]

In the very body of Christ, although our unity in a single humanity is far from complete, we have truly begun to be as closely bound to one another as we were meant to be. It is because of this very real unity with each other in Christ that we never pray alone. Of course we pray as individuals. Nevertheless always joined to our prayers are the prayers of all those who have ever been lovers of God, as well as the other Christians, living or dead, who make up the body of Christ with us. These are the prayers of Sarah and Abraham, the prayers of the prophets, Peter and James and John, of Mary the mother of Jesus, Jesus' friends Mary and Martha and Lazarus, of all the faithful Christians and sometimes martyrs of the church throughout the centuries in all places, whose lives we can only dimly imagine. Their prayers support our own.

Chapter 3

Approaching Prayer

*I*n looking at some of the sayings of our ancestors, we have begun to see into their understanding of prayer and how we might use what they teach as a lense to view prayer today. But prayer is always much more than a concept. Indeed, the monastic teachers would tell us that we cannot even understand prayer, or any other of the Christian realities, without actually trying to pray our way into them. This is why we must now give our attention to what the Abbas and Ammas have to tell us in the present about our own twentieth-century practice of prayer.

We must begin our discussion of early monastic teaching on prayer by saying absolutely emphatically: There is no one right way to pray. Nobody's way of prayer is like anyone else's.

> It was told of a brother who came to see Abba Arsenius at Scetic that, when he came to the church, he asked the clergy if he could visit Abba Arsenius.

After having a meal together they sent the visitor to Arsenius with a local brother to guide him.

> Having knocked on the door, they entered, greeted the old man and sat down without saying anything. Then the brother from the church said, "I will leave you. Pray for me." Now the visiting brother, not feeling at ease with the old man, said, "I will come with you," and they went away together. Then the visitor asked, "Take me to Abba Moses, who used to be a robber."

Where Arsenius had not so much as spoken to them, Moses was happy to see them, welcoming them warmly. An Abba who saw all this take place wondered about it, and he asked God for an explanation.

> "Lord, for Thy name's sake the one flees from [human beings], and the other, for Thy name's sake, receives them with open arms." Then two large boats were shown to him on a river and he saw Abba Arsenius and the Spirit of God sailing in the one, in perfect peace; and in the other was Abba Moses with the angels of God, and they were all eating honey cakes.[1]

Because prayer is an expression of each person's relationship to God, there is no one right way to pray. God has truly made us all different. Even if we think that there is nothing distinctive about our individual families of origin, temperaments, gifts, interests, weaknesses, they are combined in each of us in a special way. Our prayer is unique. That is why there were so many different ways of praying in the Egyptian desert.

Learning to pray means finding a way of prayer that suits us in a particular way. A friend of Anthony once asked him, "What thing is so good that I may do it and live by it?" As we saw earlier, Anthony answered not by saying, "Here is what you need to do and here is how you need to pray." Instead he answered,

> Cannot all works please God equally? Scripture says, Abraham was hospitable and God was with him. And Elijah loved quiet, and God was with him. And David was humble and God was with him. So whatever you find your soul wills in following God's will, do it, and keep your heart.[2]

No one can tell you what Christian discipline you should adopt or follow for yourself; if you are now beginning to pray for the first time, you must find for yourself what peculiarly suits you. This does not mean, however, that you must rediscover prayer for yourself in the same way you might have to rediscover the wheel if you had been abandoned at birth on an unihabited island and were raised by wolves! Our prayer is unique, but we will find it possible to talk about some common elements of the practice of prayer.

If you have been praying for a long time but feel anxiety about whether you are doing it "right," the monastic teachers remind you, "Cannot all works please God equally?" Although the Abbas and Ammas have many helpful things to say for deepening the practice and understanding of prayer, you do not need anyone to tell you the right way to pray. If you are praying, you are already "doing it right."

Not only is the prayer of each person unique. Because our shared life with God in prayer is ongoing, we need to take seriously that our prayer is going to change according to what is going on in our lives.[3] I know a woman who is trying to make sense of two dreadful occurrences in her life: she had to put her mother in a nursing home and she learned that her husband is dying of cancer. She was worried about her prayer because, although her prayer had always been a means of centering herself in God, now no matter how she prayed she could not seem to be at peace. Of course she could not! She has much in her life to assimilate, to hold God accountable for, to think through and suffer through. If she were "at peace" in her prayer, she would not be doing the basic work that is a necessary part of her growth in prayer and love both of God and her family. This woman's expectations that prayer should be the same, and that it should basically enable her to be peaceful no matter what else was happening to her, were actually keeping her from seeing that whatever our prayer is at the moment, whether it "feels" good or bad, is part of the ongoing pattern of our prayer throughout our whole lives.

As modern Christians we have some peculiar and self-destructive convictions about prayer that Christians of other periods do not always share with us. To begin with, many people believe that for real Christians both love and prayer should flow effortlessly with sincerity and spontaneity. Along with this conviction we also believe in two of its corollaries: first, if we are not sure how to pray, and love for God and for others does not flow out of us regularly with spontaneity and sincerity, we must not really be Christians. Second, if we use the words of others instead of our own flowing spontaneously from our hearts when we do pray, our prayer is not sincere. These three convictions combine to make us feel guilty, frustrated, and embarrassed because we are not more loving and we do not pray more. Vital energy in church life is then squandered trying to keep other people from finding out that we may be Christian frauds, while underneath the good fronts we put up are suffering, discouraged, and often very angry hearts.

None of this pain is necessary. Our early monastic ancestors would be baffled to think that Christians could be so unrealistic about themselves, their love, and their prayer. They knew that love and prayer, being closely related as they are, must both be learned over a whole lifetime of sincere and very often unspontaneous work on our part coupled with the continuous gift of God's grace. Even working at it a long time may not make love come easily or enable us to love everyone in the same way. Evagrius Ponticus, who had very firm notions about what human beings are potentially capable of, described for the members of his monastic community what was realistically possible for them:

> It is not possible to love all the brethren to the same degree. But it is possible to associate with all in a manner that is . . . free of resentment and hatred.[4]

For the monastics, furthermore, far from being spontaneous in our modern terms, their own very sincere prayer rested on their recitation of and meditation on the Psalms, which they believed were given to God's people partly because without them we would often be at a loss for words in prayer.

Not that early monastic prayer or love was simply the result of their own hard work and determination. Evagrius spoke of prayer as the gift of God, and all of them believed that whenever we are present to God in our prayer and God is present to us, it is always by the gift of God's grace rather than the result of something that we do.

For many modern Christians the notion of "learning" either to pray or to love is startling. This is especially so for the families of Protestantism, who historically have stressed the insignificance of human work compared to the depth of the gift of God's grace. At the same time they have emphasized that as we are all sinners, anything good we do—such as loving or praying—is a gift of God that naturally flows from us out of God's original gift to us of our salvation. All we can contribute is our faith, for "salvation [is] by faith, alone."

In its modern form this insight goes back to the Reformation. After being tangled up in his own overscrupulous conscience and suffering a great deal from it, while he was pondering Paul's Letter to the Romans, Martin Luther came to understand that he did not need to struggle over sin because salvation is a gift of God's grace and not something we earn by being good people. This insight of Luther's was enormously freeing to him, and it became one of the fundamental theological principles of the Reformation. We are saved by grace through faith and not by works; works then flow out of faith.

But many people have inherited Luther's insight in a distorted form that makes them suspicious of anything hinting that "works" might affect our salvation, to the extent that they believe love and prayer must flow from the heart of the Christian without any special effort. Talk about learning to love and learning to pray or using the prayers of others for our own prayers suggests to them a failure to understand that our salvation does indeed spring from faith in God alone.

Our early monastic relatives would be confused. Of course, they would say, salvation is the gift of God to us; it is true that salvation is partly a matter of God loving us and accepting us as we are, but it also has a great deal to do with growing in love and prayer in the Christian life. If we mean by "salvation" God's love and acceptance of us, we certainly do nothing to earn it. If we use "salvation" to include our Christian growth in God, this growth is not something that is given to us all at once without our doing anything to bring it about. We are given the image of God at our creation, and it is never totally erased; it remains within us as a need and ability to respond to God's saving grace and even to seek out God's grace, which God has promised will be given to us over and over throughout our lives as we grow in the Christian life.[5]

There is nothing mysterious about how we respond to this grace. Suppose that my relationship with a coworker has been tense lately. When I arrive at work this morning, my fellow worker snaps irritably at me over nothing in particular. My teenager had earlier hurt my feelings, and I have not had such a good morning myself. I would like to rush into my office and brood over my injuries while I nurse my anger. But I know I should work at restoring my relationship with the coworker, no matter how good my anger feels. Granted that there are situations and relationships in which we need to get angry in order to bring about changes, this situation is straightforward. I have a choice. Giving in to one set of feelings will result in immediate gratification and will be easy; the other set of feelings may involve me in an embarrassing conversation or worse. In this situation the nagging feeling that we ought not give in to our anger but rather try to resolve it is an offer of the gift of God's reconciling grace; an apology from the offending party is another. In both cases, God will not provide a reconciliation on my behalf without my choosing to respond and to act appropriately.

As for prayer, God's grace comes together with our response as surely as they come together every place else in our lives. The secret of seeing it is to be found by realizing that the interchange of grace and response do not remain within the prayer alone. Prayer and life must be all of a piece. As Abba Moses once said,

> If a [person's] deeds are not in harmony with his [or her] prayer, [that person] labors in vain. The brother said, "What is this harmony between practice and prayer?" The old man said "We should no longer do those things against which we pray."[6]

Suppose I am perpetually angry with a neighbor who seems to have nothing better to do than to harass the people who live on her street. I pray for help in forgiving my obnoxious neighbor and the ability to treat her, as Evagrius says, "without resentment and hatred."[7] Perhaps during the course of my prayer I receive an insight into the neighbor, or myself, that allows me to see her differently. That insight is a gift of grace. It is not so compelling, however, that I will have to relate differently to her in the future. I can have the insight, continue to nurse a grudge, and end up angrier than ever. Or I may carry my insight out of my prayer, ponder it, and bring myself to begin a friendly conversation with her that may make compassion toward her even more possible. No one who has had this very ordinary and everyday experience will have any illusions about gritting the teeth and forgiving as an effort of will. It simply is not possible without grace. Yet when grace comes, we must be waiting to respond by our actions and by our further prayer.

The early church took Paul seriously when he said:

> the Spirit . . . comes to help us in our weakness, for, when we do not know how to pray properly, then the Spirit personally makes our petitions for us in groans that cannot be put into words; and [the one] who can see into all hearts knows what the Spirit means.[8]

Evagrius took Paul further; it is not only when we do not know how to pray that the Spirit helps us;

> If you wish to pray then it is God whom you need. [God] it is who gives prayer to the [one] who prays.[9]

All the monastic teachers believed that, although we must learn to pray, still, whenever we are present to God in our prayer and God is present to us, it is always by the gift of God's grace rather than the result of something we do.

In the final analysis prayer is paradoxically both something we learn to do and a gift given to us by God that we must receive. Much of the following advice on the practice of prayer might seem too ordinary, too much a part of the daily round of simple activities that often threatens to consume our lives rather than bring us closer to God. In taking up the practice of prayer, however, we must always bear in mind that first and last, prayer is a pursuit of the God who has promised us God's own self, not just for the time of prayer but always. Thus our activity becomes a way of responding to God's grace. Even the stern Arsenius tells us,

> "If we seek God, [God] will appear to us: if we hold [God], [God] will stay with us."[10]

With all this in mind, let us look now at some important elements of the practice of prayer: finding a time to pray; our disposition when praying; Scripture and prayer; praying in silence and in conversation; religious experience; and the importance of persistence in prayer.

TIME TO PRAY

Beginning to pray takes a commitment to a countercultural way of looking at life. It is countercultural to spend time every day doing something that we claim is valuable and yet not "productive." We live in a society that believes in being productive. In our world of consumer values those who do not produce tend to be regarded almost as nonpeople: children, the old, the handicapped, the unemployed, street people, the very poor, housewives—all are treated as though they are of little consequence among us. We value ourselves and each other in terms of what we contribute concretely to our job, which in turn benefits the whole of the society in which we live. Even leisure time is valued as time spent resting in order to allow us to work well and continue contributing. I have heard ministers say with a little pride in their voices that because they never take time off, they naturally do not have time for daily prayer. Once a minister told me that she could not use her church office for her prayer because her congregation would not put up with her praying on the church's time; they pay her to do a job, not to pray.

Many people say that they would like to take the time to pray every day, but when it comes down to do it, it makes them feel selfish. How can they justify doing something so entirely for themselves while there are so many things that need to get done? Strangely, people who have no difficulty reading or watching television without thinking of themselves as selfish are entirely undone by the attempt to claim time to pray.

Once you decide to spend a little time every day in prayer, you may find that you have much more of one or both of these attitudes yourself than you might think. You may experience a reluctance on your part to take the time because it seems as though time for prayer is time away from the real business of life. Once having taken the time, you may apologize in your head to the rest of the family for not being with them during your prayer, or you may feel guilty not coming to the phone if you receive a call during your prayers.

You may be tempted to deal with this uneasiness by telling yourself that prayer is productive for you or good for you even though nobody can see it, because you "get so much out of it." At the very outset let me caution you about giving in to this temptation to describe prayer in these terms. Prayer is fundamentally being in connection with God. Good things may and do come out of it, but we do not pray for the sake of those good things. If we pray primarily to "get something out of it," whether it is psychic wholeness, insight into our own depths, or a new bicycle, we are giving up the goal of love of God before we even start. How can we love God if we only approach God in terms of what God can or will give us?

Moreover, if you tell yourself you pray for what you get out of it, you may come to think that the only prayer that is good or sincere or real is prayer in which you experience something very vividly. But living in an intentional relationship with God in prayer is like living in a happy marriage. When a person is first in love, the beloved is constantly on the mind, and time spent in the other person's presence can have an almost hallucinatory quality. The one in love has a heightened sense of the self and the lover in which every minute counts, and the other's every word and gesture seem full of meaning. It is magical while it lasts, and it is always remembered. If this initial love is to grow into the nourishing and long-term love of a good marriage, however, the way lovers come to be together on a day-to-day basis has to change of itself. The intensely focused times continue, but the two come to spend far more time together when nothing productive appears to be happening; they read the paper together, do the dishes, eat a meal, and this shared, very ordinary, everyday time becomes a fundamental and very necessary part of the precious foundation of the marriage, in which love infuses all that the lovers do together.

For many people, beginning to pray regularly is like falling in love, and prayer for them often also has a very focused, very intense quality to it. Like first falling in love, it is wonderful. Nevertheless if you believe that what you "get out of" prayer depends on having an intense experience in prayer, when that focused quality begins to fall away, you may come to believe that you are no longer truly praying when just the opposite is probably true: You are entering into the deep and solid life of everyday prayer that is equivalent to the precious ordinary time in marriage. The danger of confusing "a religious experience," which may in fact be a product of your own unconcious mind, with prayer is what this funny story is about:

> The demons, wanting to seduce an old man, said to him: "Would you like to see Christ?" He said: "A curse be upon you and him of whom you speak. I believe my Christ when he said: 'If anyone says to you, Lo, here is Christ, or Lo, there, do not believe him.' " And they vanished at the words.[11]

Lest you be shocked at the cursing, the old man is not cursing Christ, whom he knows he cannot see, but whatever it might be that would appear to him as Christ through the work of the demons.

When it comes to selecting a daily time for prayer, it is important to remember that prayer, like any family life, needs regular time. Do not choose a time that, realistically speaking, you will not be able to sustain on a daily basis, like four o'clock in the morning (unless you ordinarily are up then anyway.) Select a time when you know you will be able to pray every day; after breakfast or the late afternoon or before bed are the times that work for most people. If you are the parent of a baby or a preschool child, it may be hard to find an uninterrupted time when you are still awake enough to be able to pray. Flexibility helps. Decide that you will pray between breakfast and lunch or supper and bedtime or between any other regular activities you engage in. It is easier to pick one stretch of time and stick to it than to tell yourself simply that you will pray sometime during the day. It is hard to allow prayer to become part of your ordinary daily life if there is no set time for it.

Choose a quiet place in your house or office; if you need to, take the phone off the hook and put a Do Not Disturb sign on your door. You may have older children or a spouse or both; ask them not to speak with you during this time. Clearly you cannot turn a toddler loose in the house or let a baby cry for twenty minutes. Short of these, however, if you believe your prayer is important for you, others will usually find that rarely is something so important that you must be interrupted.

If you do miss your prayers because you have company or your child has the flu or because you oversleep or you have some emergency, say them when you can. This was a problem that came up in the desert, too.

A brother asked one of the fathers: "If by chance I oversleep, and am late for the hour of prayer, I am ashamed that others will hear me praying so late, and so I become reluctant to keep the rule of prayer." And the old man said: "If ever you oversleep the dawn, rise when you wake, shut the door and the windows, and say your [prayers]. For it is written 'The day is thine and the night is thine.' God is glorified whatever time it is."[12]

The Abba in this story tells the embarrassed brother to shut the door and windows so that he need not have to worry about what his brothers think. Many people feel guilty if they move the time of their prayers or even miss their prayers. Make things easy on yourself, as the Abba did for the brother. Remember that you are not praying to fulfill a religious obligation laid on you from the outside or for the reward of becoming a "good person."

After you have chosen a realistic time of day, set a realistic length of time for your prayers as well, perhaps twenty minutes to a half hour. It is helpful to listen to the advice of Anthony to young monastics who were praying several times a day anyway and on top of it felt driven to be overzealous in their prayer and monastic disciplines. Anthony speaks of demons where we might be more comfortable speaking of feeling driven by something within ourselves, but the effect is the same:

"While we are sleeping [the demons] arouse us for prayers, and they do this incessantly, hardly allowing us to sleep. . . . They do not do these things for the sake of piety or truth, but so that they might bring the simple to despair."[13]

Most of us do not live in monasteries. Most people who decide to spend an unrealistically long time in prayer quickly despair and come to believe that prayer is not for them because they cannot discipline themselves or take the time.

It is helpful to understand that regularity is more sustaining in prayer than intensity or length. You are spending time with God, learning who God is and who you are, learning to love God and God's world, and this happens over a matter of years. If you miss some days, start again, and think small. A brother told an Abba that he had gotten away from his monastic disciplines, presumably including his prayer, and he felt too discouraged to begin again. The Abba replied by telling him this story:

> "A man had a plot of land. And through his carelessness brambles sprang up and it became a wilderness of thistles and thorns. Then he decided to cultivate it. So he said to his son: 'Go and clear that ground.' So the son went to clear it, and saw that the thistles and thorns had multiplied. . . . He said: 'How much time shall I need to clear and weed all this?' And he lay on the ground and went to sleep. He did this day after day. Later his father came to see what he had done, and found him doing nothing."

When his father asked him about it, the son replied that the job looked so bad that he could never make himself begin. His father replied,

> " 'Son, if you had cleared each day the area on which you lay down, your work would have advanced slowly and you would not have lost heart.' So the lad did what his father said, and in a short time the plot was cultivated."

So the Abba told the discouraged brother,

> "Do a little work and do not faint, and God will give you grace."[14]

The disheartened brother took up his prayer again with patience without trying to do everything. You can, too. Prayer is for you. Prayer is not a test of your character, an endurance contest, or a heroic task set before you.

DISPOSITIONS FOR PRAYER

Once you have chosen a time and place for prayer and decided on a realistic length for it, you may find other states within yourself that seem to make your prayer difficult or even impossible. Most of these come under the heading of attitudes that seem unsuitable for prayer: you are angry, or sleepy, or feeling frivolous, or unable to concentrate.

If you find yourself thinking in these terms, there is a good chance that you believe—perhaps unwittingly—you must be "worthy" of God, and that God is only interested in your "good" self. Think about it. If this is indeed what you believe, how could you ever love such a God? You will surely find prayer a dreadful burden. This is the despair Luther felt before his insight. Ask yourself if you are using prayer to get yourself to "be good," to coerce yourself, for example, to stay or be happy in a job, or a marriage, or a relationship you hate. If you are, you are committing an act of violence on yourself in God's name. Many children are taught to pray this way: "God, make me love my little brother" or "Help me make all A's in school." It is no wonder they very often hate anything to do with religion as adults.

We need to bring ourselves to our prayer just as we are—bored, sleepy, distracted, mad, happy. As Psalm 139 says, God knows us most thoroughly anyway. That we can be utterly ourselves in God's presence as we may not feel we can be in anyone else's is one of the greatest gifts of prayer. Remember, it was the "good" people Jesus had a hard time being around, not the "difficult" or the "bad," and these difficult included his own disciples whom he had chosen himself. Even the disciples' argument about who would sit at Jesus' right and left hand did not drive Jesus away, although he must have felt a little discouraged about what they had understood of his preaching and deeds.

You may find being who you are in God's presence something very hard to learn. It may even be hard to recognize that you would prefer God not to see your mean or lazy or nonreligious side, and so you try to present an idealized self to God. Our monastic brothers and sisters must have had this difficulty themselves. I think this was what Poemen was addressing when he said,

To throw yourself before God, not to measure your progress, to leave behind all self-will; these are the instruments for the work of the soul.[15]

All three of the elements of this saying tell us to leave the business of judging our worthiness to God, who surely loves us as we are, as Jesus did.

Nevertheless we are right in knowing that love and prayer go together in such a way that as angry as we may be at another person or situation as we go into prayer, we must leave the judgment of that person or situation to God. This does not mean, however, that we pretend we do not have feelings we really have or that we do have feelings we do not. Instead we must enter prayer honestly and fully as who we are at the moment. We will be coming back to what we do with our anger in two other chapters.[16]

Sometimes who we are at the moment is people whose minds are wandering away from our prayer and onto all sorts of other things, such as what we will have for dinner tonight or our unpaid pile of bills. How can we pray then? Are we not insulting God and wasting our time? Ought we not just quit when we catch ourselves, and try again at a more suitable time? Or worse, perhaps we are people who cannot pray? This problem, too, we share with our desert ancestors, and the Abbas had a good answer to it:

A brother asked an old man and said: "My thoughts wander, and I am troubled." He answered: "Go on sitting in your cell, and your thoughts will come back from their wanderings. If a she-ass is tethered, her foal skips and gambols all round her but always comes back to the mother. So it will be with the [person] who for God's sake sits patiently in his [or her] cell. Though [the] thoughts wander for a time, they will come again."[17]

As the little donkey comes back to its mother, our minds, too, will return to God in our prayer, and even if they do not, we are in God's presence just the same. If we are there exactly as we are, there will be times, probably a lot of times, when our minds will wander. It is always better to be in God's presence in the way we can be than not to be there at all.

There is one more caution to be made about our disposition going into prayer. Many people are accustomed to going through their days continually reproaching themselves for what they perceive to be their failures: "I never can make myself get up for my prayers; I am no good," as well as "I cannot believe I yelled at the children; I am a terrible mother," or, "I never answer my letters on time; no one else is this irresponsible." If you do this, it will truly hinder your prayer. You are taking on yourself the role of God against yourself, but you are not treating yourself as God in fact treats you. You are exercising violence, while God treats all of us gently, never forcing or bullying us, or riding roughshod over us.

> It is not possible for a [person] to be recalled from his [or her] purpose by harshness and severity—demon cannot drive out demon: you will bring him back to you better by kindness. That is how God acts for our good, and draws us to [God's self].[18]

The Abba's advice about dealing with the brother is that violence does not work on a practical level; what does work is the kind of gentleness God exercises. It can take a great deal of vigilance to follow monastic advice on this matter. Nevertheless I believe that the monastics were right. We need to cultivate the discipline of giving up violence to the self in exchange for God's gentleness if we are to grow in prayer and love as well.

Some of us who deeply distrust our own and others' motivations may worry that such an emphasis on the image of God will make us "think too much of ourselves." Perhaps we will stop taking our own sin seriously and become naive optimists who no longer look out for others. Perhaps we will become totally irresponsible if we do not keep ourselves in line by a certain roughness toward ourselves.

These worries can be put to rest if we remember why it is that we are giving up such violence against the self: It is out of our own respect for the image of God within us, out of gratitude toward God for the gift of the image, and out of the knowledge that love of God and others cannot grow from self-hatred. The answer to the rest of these worries lies in our expectation of our prayer, based as it is in Scripture and shared with the whole of the people of God. We must act in trust that this prayer, which is the gift of God to all God's people, will shape us and conform us to God's love.

In fact the early monastics consistently claimed that as we grow in the life of love of God and neighbor, we grow more, rather than less, aware of our own sin. Such an awareness did not produce self-hatred. Instead it served the purpose of love. In chapter 5 we will see how, as the sisters' or brothers' sensitivity to their own sin grew, so did their ability to identify with and love the sinner, no matter what that sin was.

SCRIPTURE

Scripture was the backbone of monastic prayer. This is because the Abbas and Ammas knew that if prayer is shared life with God, one of the most fundamental ways God shares God's self with us is in the Bible. If Christians truly want to listen to the voice of God, praying Scripture is a basic way we listen. Our early Christian ancestors considered Scripture to be one of God's most precious gifts to God's people. For them it embodied divine truth and love, a record of God's revelation of God's self, especially in Jesus. It presented to them both a picture of what they wanted to become in Christ and the way to it, if they could live it out. This is why when illiterate new recruits came to the monasteries of Pachomius[19] they were immediately put to work learning to read Scripture. Epipanius said,

"Ignorance of the Scriptures is a precipice and a deep abyss."[20]

If it is true that we are formed by our prayer, it is particularly true that we are formed by praying Scripture. Abba Poemen, who had great faith in the slow but steady power of Scripture wrestled with over time, said,

"The nature of water is soft, that of stone is hard; but if a bottle is hung above the stone, allowing the water to fall drop by drop, it wears away the stone. So it is with the word of God; it is soft and our heart is hard, but the [person] who hears the word of God often opens [the] heart to the fear of God."[21]

For the monks and for us as well this process of being formed by the word of God happens not so much by our conscious effort as by our daily steeping in it, until it becomes as familiar and natural to us as the language we speak.

The starting point of desert prayer was the Psalms both for public and private prayer. Our Christian ancestors regarded the Psalms as unique in the Bible. They believed that the Psalms contained the entire Bible in miniature, but the real uniqueness of the Psalms lay in the fact that they were themselves prayers given by

God the Holy Spirit to be spoken as our own words in our own particular situations. Athanasius, the great fourth-century theologian and bishop of Alexandria, who was the special friend of the monks, says about the Psalms:

> Each psalm is both spoken and composed by the Spirit so that in these same words . . . the stirring of our souls might be grasped, and all of them be said as concerning us, and [the Psalms] issue from us as our own words.[22]

What in particular do the Psalms do for us? First, suggests Althanasius, often when we pray we do not recognize what is going on in our deepest selves. The words of the Psalms, however, have the power as we pray them to "become like a mirror to the person singing them."[23] Often by praying a psalm expressing anger or grief or happiness or guilt the person doing the praying becomes able both to recognize and to express her or his deepest and most heartfelt emotions and convictions.

Second, although it is important to know what we feel and to be able to express it both to ourselves and God, often when we pray the Psalms in this way, they are able to stand over against us. Thus, at the same time that we are able to recognize our emotions and convictions we also become able to see how these convictions and the attitudes and behavior that result from them are hurting us. In this case, says Athanasius, the Psalms in a special way also offer insight into what we want and need instead. This insight itself becomes the source of healing. Thus, Athanasius says,

> just as [God] provided the model of the earthly and heavenly [person] in [God's] own person, so also from the Psalms he [or she] who wants to do so can learn the emotions and dispositions of the soul, finding in them also the therapy and correction suited for each emotion.[24]

Those who make the Psalms part of their daily prayer find that Athanasius is right. The Psalms do very often seem to have the ability to help us recognize ourselves and the self-inflicted distortions we live with in very specific ways, and they continue to have the ability to touch us at a very deep level, shaking loose destructive ways of seeing and relating to God, ourselves, and our world.

Often when people begin to pray the Psalms they find them full of images of violence and vengeance. It is helpful to know how fourth- and fifth-century commentators on these texts handled them. Knowing that God wants the good of every creature, they did not believe the Psalms were invoking God's rage against real human beings. Instead the enemies seemed to these early Christian writers to be our own internal enemies, habits of thoughts, obsessions, and false evaluations of ourselves, to which we are enslaved. Obviously the fourth- and fifth-century writers were wrong about the original intent of the writers. Nevertheless, for the purposes of prayer, they were right. For many people, to be able to address those internal destructive forces by means of praying the Psalms is a wonderful gift.

This process of addressing what is internally destructive can sometimes take a very long time and can work in a most complex way. A woman I know who is accustomed to praying the Psalms daily told me that one summer several years ago she suddenly became aware of feeling terribly wounded by the enormous number of male pronouns, the male imagery, and particularly the warrior imagery in the Psalms. The language of the Psalms not only made her feel excluded and repulsed, it also made her painfully aware of the ambiguities toward women in the world at large and in the Christian tradition itself. Along with her growing awareness of her specific pain, she became angry with God as she prayed. Why was God on the side of the successful? This was Scripture! In growing pain and anger she continued to ask God for help over several weeks. Her help finally came. One day when she began her Psalms, she was able really to hear in Psalm 72 what she had never heard before:

> The Anointed delivers the needy when they call;
> The poor and those who are helpless,
> Having pity on the weak and the needy,
> saving the lives of the poor.
> From oppression and violence they are redeemed;
> and precious is their blood.[25]

She was able to hear God speak at last: "Whatever you may hear, I do not prefer those with power. I am in a special way the God of those society disregards, of the oppressed, of the old, the poor, the powerless. Whatever anyone may say, you are made in my image. I want your wholeness. I want you to thrive. When you fight for yourself, you fight with me behind you." At this point she began in her prayers to ponder over Jesus and what kind of people he associated with and died for. This was a real turning point. Up until then she had not known if she could even remain Christian. For the first time she felt confident in her ability to work in the church.

How do I pray any part of Scripture so that I am able to hear it speak in this way? The Abbas and Ammas do not recommend a special technique.[26] First, however, I begin knowing that although the Bible comes from a time and place and culture very different from my own, God means it to speak to me in the present. When I pray, I know that Scripture is not meant to be about what was; it is for God's people at this moment. I listen to Scripture in whatever way I can, not for a literal description of what was and will be but for the stories, metaphors, and images of God and God's people that ask me to be a part of them right now.[27] The fifth-century author of the *Macarian Homilies* gives a particularly beautiful ancient example of this listening:

> When you hear that at that time the Lord freed the souls from hell and the regions of darkness and that He descended into hell and did an amazing work, do not think that this does not have any personal meaning for you. [Human beings], indeed, can readily take and receive the evil one. Death has its grip on the children of Adam and their thoughts are imprisoned in darkness. And when you hear mention of tombs, do not at once think only of visible ones. For your heart is a tomb and a sepulcher. When the prince of evil and his angels have built their nest there and have built roads and highways on which the powers of Satan walk about inside your mind . . . are you not a hell and . . . a tomb, dead to God?
>
> For there it was that Satan stamped out counterfeit coins of silver. In such a soul he sowed bitter seeds. He leavened it with old leaven. There is where a murky, muddy fountain flows. But the Lord descends into the souls of those who seek Him; He goes into the depths of the hellish heart and there He commands death, saying: "Release those captive souls that seek after Me, those that you hold by force in bondage." He, therefore, breaks through the heavy stones that cover the soul. He opens the tombs. He truly raises to life the dead person and leads that captive soul forth out of the dark prison.[28]

I also pray in the expectation that the words of Scripture are there to bring life and not death. This means that when I encounter something there that demoralizes me or makes me feel isolated from God, from other people, or from myself, I know that this is not God's intent. One place many people—both men and women— experience such demoralization and separation is in the way they hear the overwhelmingly masculine language of Scripture, which often seems to assume that both God and God's people are exclusively male.

That God wants our wholeness is the principle that allows us to set aside those passages in Scripture that would appear to work against us. As the Bible is God's word for us in the present, it is also important to remember that it comes to us out of an ancient and alien Near Eastern culture. This means that in many places we find contradictions in the Bible. While it calls us to freedom, wholeness, and the new creation, it also accepts the mores of that ancient culture, over against God's word of life, including not only the subordination of women but slavery as well. If we cannot accept the whole of the Bible as it stands, how do we know what to accept? Jesus said and lived out in his own relationships, "I have come to bring you life."[29] God does not want our spirits broken or our blind obedience to whatever is. Praying Scripture is for my life. This means that if I feel myself shut out when Paul addresses the people of God as "brothers," I add in my praying "and sisters." When I pray Psalm 1, "Blessed is the man who . . ." I change it to "Blessed is the person who . . ." and I have no qualms about it.

What about the names for God? Most of us in our prayer are stuck in a very limited number of "religious" names and images for God—Father, Lord, Savior, Mighty, for example—that narrows our ability to know God in more than the few ways we have known God since childhood. In some cases, if as children and even adults we associate God with important figures of authority in our lives who have hurt us, to pray to God using those names can do us injury. Not only does it limit our ability to know God in other and truer ways, it also keeps us from the healing love God intends for us. Where we know we are being hurt, in our private prayer we avoid those names, no matter how hallowed the tradition.

At the same time, in praying Scripture daily we work hard to get to know the God of the Bible, a God who is infinitely complex and many faceted, mysterious, and at the same time intimately loving. We meditate on what kind of God can be described as "living water" for us. We try to hear deeply who our God really is when Hosea describes God as a gentle father who did not think it beneath him to teach baby Israel to walk. We ask to know the one who cares about us so much that our names should be written on the palm of God's hand.

While we are learning all this, we also begin to understand in our hearts the importance of the truth that so many writers of the early church fought for: God is so infinitely inexhaustible that none of the names Scripture gives to God, not even all of them put together, can ever finally define God. Whether we pray to God as our peace, rock, mother, wisdom, water of life, father, maker of the world, Spirit, friend, healer, comforter, redeemer, great bird[30]— all these names are finally provisional. The God we come to love who is our light, our life, and our joy is wonderfully beyond us.[31]

Is this all finally a matter of my own private tastes? In the end do I simply pick and choose what suits me best? The Abbas and Ammas remind us that even in prayer the interpretation of Scripture is always shared. Because Athanasius and the author of the *Macarian Homilies* recommend allowing Scripture in prayer to be our own, one might be tempted to believe that they also thought that each person is equally able to interpret Scripture in any circumstances with no more help than the Holy Spirit. This is not the position of anyone in the early church. The Bible is the book of the church; it was given to the church for the upbuilding of the whole body of Christ, and it has been preserved in the church. Totally private interpretation of Scripture was no more possible to our fourth century Christian ancestors than was a totally private relationship to God that was not lived out in a Christian community and expressed as love of others in God's larger world. A nice story in the *Sayings* illustrates what happened when a brother tried to get God to give him the interpretation of a tough passage in Scripture:

> They said of an old man that he went on fasting for seventy weeks, eating a meal only once a week. He asked of God the meaning of a text of the holy Scriptures and God did not reveal it to him. So he said to himself: "Here I am: I have worked so hard, and profited nothing. I will go to my brother and ask him." Just as he had shut his door on the way out, an angel of the Lord was sent to him; and the angel said: "The seventy weeks of your fast have not brought you near to God: but now you are humbled and going to your brother, I have been sent to show you the meaning of the text." And he explained to him what he had asked, and went away.[32]

Finally, we must remember that the Bible is not a book of secret messages. It is God's word for our hearts and for our life together, but in a good many cases it is not self-explanatory. If we believe that we never need help in understanding Scripture, we suffer from the same arrogance the brother in this story had. We need to know everything we can about it if it is to be life giving to us in the way it can be. "Going to ask the brothers and sisters" in our time means drawing on the resources available to us in our Christian life together and returning to our prayer alone enriched by the resources we have shared together.

SILENCE IN PRAYER

Ongoing conversation with God is a very important part of prayer. If we are to share our lives with God, we must be willing to tell God explicitly what we have on our minds, whether we believe it "suitable" or not, as well as ask for what we want and need for ourselves, God's people, and God's world. Conversation with God can take many shapes. It does not have to be in the form of many words. To lift up the image of a person's face to God in intercessions or simply to say to God, "I am angry that you put me in this situation" is very often enough. Conversation can take the form of writing in a journal or jotting down images. But real conversation cannot consist in one person or even two people constantly talking. We often forget that any real conversation needs silence.

It is a commonplace that we do not live in a culture that makes much place for silence. In many households the radio, TV, or stereo is on constantly. We seem to associate sound and "doing something useful." We are afraid of what we might feel or think about if we are left with only ourselves in our own silence. Even our worship services are like this. We move from one part to another without leaving space just to be in the presence of God and each other. For the fathers and mothers of the ancient Egyptian desert, silence was also excruciating difficult, so difficult, in fact, that

> it was said of Abba Agathon that for three years he lived with a stone in his mouth, until he had learnt to keep silence.[33]

Silence was essential to the life and prayer of the monk. While our silence cannot be as systematic and extensive as theirs, I believe that silence has a very important place in our own daily prayer.

We pray in silence with the monks in three different ways. The first we have already encountered in our discussion of Scripture.

If we wish to hear God speak, a primary way we know we will hear the voice of God is in the words of the Bible. If we are to pray Scripture, rather than simply tell ourselves and God what we think it says, we listen to its words and then sit in silence in its presence to let it come alive in us in our depths. Whether this silence is only for a few moments or for much longer times, I believe it is always a necessary part of praying Scripture.

A different kind of silence in prayer in the ancient desert was "imageless prayer," or "pure prayer." In its most austere form it was associated with the fourth-century teacher Evagrius Ponticus.[34] For Evagrius this kind of prayer came only at the end of a discipline that lasted many years, during which one learned to control the passions and become a fully loving person. As Evagrius speaks of it, "pure prayer" entails being in the presence of God without in any way visualizing or conceptualizing God. At the same time the mind must also be empty of all other thoughts of ordinary life. Thus, Evagrius tell his disciples,

> You will not be able to pray purely if you are all involved with material affairs and agitated with unremitting concerns. For prayer is the rejection of concepts.[35]

In this respect Evagrius's pure prayer is like Zen meditation. In the Book of Isaiah God says, "My ways are not your ways, nor my thoughts your thoughts." Where in other places in prayer the monks experienced God's intimacy with us in our everyday life, the point of this kind of prayer was a kind of knowing God by knowing what God is not. In this way the monk was to come to know God intimately in God's utterly loving "otherness" to all things created.

Pure prayer was not for most monks in the ancient world, let alone for most of us. One of its modern relatives, however, often called "centering prayer,"[36] has proved to be helpful to many Christians of our own time. The basis of this form of prayer is the use of a short prayer phrase, such as "Lord have mercy,"[37] which one repeats during the space of time one draws in and breathes out one breath. Meanwhile the person praying simply sits in the presence of God, having let go of every expectation of self and God, of who the self is or ought to be, and even of who God is or ought to be. As is the case with Evagrius's pure prayer, this is a way of learning to know God by negation—of coming to know God by learning who God is not. For people who are very bound by "oughts" and who are much more aware of God as judge than God as lover and healer, this kind of prayer can be very freeing.

On the other hand, centering prayer is rather formal. For some people it is the basic stuff of their prayer, while many others find it impossible. There is a related but much more informal way of being in God's presence, however, that almost everyone finds deeply nourishing as part of their daily prayer. Although it is not a monastic term at all, I like to think of it as kitchen table prayer. It is good to spend time with our friends or spouse talking. A vital part of the truly intimate relationships we have with the people we love best does not involve talking at all. Kitchen table prayer is time we spend with God that is like time we spend at the kitchen table with a spouse or a good friend with whom we share our lives in other ways already. When we pray like this we simply sit in silence. Sometimes it is peaceful; sometimes it is distracted; sometimes we even fall asleep, but it is always shared. This time spent with God is not listening; it does not need attentiveness; it is sitting in each other's loving presence, glad to be together, whatever else is going on. However else we pray, I believe that this daily period of silence in which we expect nothing of God and ask for nothing brings life to the prayer of every Christian.

RELIGIOUS EXPERIENCE

Now let us turn to another kind of issue in the daily practice of prayer. While it is never the case for a large number of Christians, many people who take up a discipline of prayer find themselves having experiences that fall outside of the everyday. An intense experience of the presence of God; a powerful dream; vividly experienced words or images during prayer; an unexpected emotional response; a sudden insight that seems to come from nowhere—all fall within this category. The early monastic teachers also had these experiences, and what to make of them was a heated topic in the desert.

On the one hand, warnings like this one abound in the *Sayings* to distrust all religious experience:

They said of another old man, that while he was undergoing temptation in his cell, he saw the demons face to face, and was contemptuous of them. The devil, seeing himself overcome, came and showed himself, saying: "I am Christ." The old man looked at him and shut his eyes. The devil said: "I am Christ, so why have you shut your eyes?" The old man answered: "I would not see Christ in this life, but in the next." And the devil vanished at the words.[38]

The Abbas and Ammas were acutely aware of the human ability to have "religious experiences" that never came from God, not only false visions of God, as in this saying, but also false insight into Scripture and false pangs of conscience.[39] If the monastics took these experiences seriously, they could be harmful in a number of ways, such as urging him or her to suicide or murder. The most common worry, however, was that the experience would encourage the monk to believe that God had set him or her apart for special revelation so that he or she was both superior to and no longer in need of the rest of the community.[40]

Even an experience that the Abbas and Ammas regarded as truly coming from God, however, they were cautious about. This is because it always carried with it the danger that those who received it would thereby think they had a truer or more special relationship to God than their brothers and sisters or that they knew more of the truth. So we find in the *Sayings* stories illustrating the destruction of monks that result from true revelations of God as well as false[41] and a general climate that warns not to seek religious experience of any sort.

On the other hand, the monastic literature is also full of accounts of true and highly valued religious experiences. Some of these are dreams or visions that offer insight into a particular situation.[42] Others were truly life changing, as when Dorotheos was permanently freed of his fears.[43] Still others seem to have had ecstatic union with God that the teachers are unable or unwilling to describe.[44]

From all this we can learn for our own prayer. Above all, the Abbas and Ammas teach us never simply to take a religious experience at face value and let it be. First, we must seriously question whether or not it is of God. Second, it must be thought through and evaluated, in some cases over a very long time. It is not enough simply to experience it. If it is of God, it must be integrated into who we are and how we love on an everyday level, otherwise even if it is from God, it will be lost.

If we have a powerful religious experience, we need always to remember that just because a religious experience is powerful it is not necessarily from God. Under various kinds of external and internal stresses and desires, the mind is capable of producing all sorts of things. For the monks the truth of each experience had to be tested, and the primary ancient test was love. Does this experience make us feel singled out and either superior or not accountable to others in or out of the community because of it? Does it suggest that there are goals higher in life than love, like honor or self-fulfillment or vengeance? Does it lead us to be judgmental of others, to say who deserves to belong to God's people and who does not? If the goal of the Christian life is love, that which destroys love is by definition not of God.

Or does this experience give us insight into ourselves, others, or God that furthers love? Does it give us strength or compassion toward ourselves or other people? Do its insights hold good over a long period of time, or was it simply an emotional high that not only wears off but makes us seek another? Does integrating it into ourselves change our ways of seeing, feeling, and thinking?

A middle-aged friend of mine told me about his prayer discipline one Lent. He had always been at odds with his mother, but a recent visit with her had convinced him that he needed for her sake, if not for his, to make peace with her. He resolved to use his prayer during Lent to go through his earliest memories to try to come to some of the sources of their antagonism. Over the course of the first week, he discovered that he felt a real hatred toward the child he was, and he recognized that his warfare with his mother was connected with it. After praying for several weeks for help with this hatred, he found a very strong image in his mind one morning: He was swimming under water when a little child whom he knew to be himself swam up under him and threw its arms and legs around his body. He told me he was suddenly filled with love for this child and was convinced that he could care for the child as well. From that time, he says, his hatred toward the child he was has been permanently dissolved.

The original impetus of his prayer, however, was toward the healing of his relationship with his mother. Although the original experience was the gift of God, God does not do our thinking for us. Over several years of reflecting upon and praying through the meaning of his experience, his relationship with his mother has been healed. The sure sign that his experience was truly the gift of God is that reflecting on it is still giving him new insights and help in learning to love God, other people, and God's world.

There is one final monastic insight that we need for our prayer. Abba Sisoes said,

Seek God, and do not seek where [God] dwells.[45]

It is a great temptation to seek out religious experience. The monastic teachers were convinced, however, that this is always a mistake. On the one hand, it is simply too easy to substitute a desire for a religious experience for a desire for God. No matter how powerful an experience it is, God is not an experience. Whether one has religious experiences or not probably is a matter of temperament and personality. No one, the monastics believed, needs to have religious experiences in order to have a real relationship with God. Prayer is a shared life with God. What we need most is to learn to live in an ordinary, everyday, even routine way with the God we are learning to love.

PERSISTENCE AND FORTITUDE

Prayer is shared life with God over an entire lifetime. Within this shared life we grow into the measure of the image of God, the companion of God we were intended to be. Whatever else we do or are, in order for this to happen we need the related fundamental monastic virtues: persistence and fortitude. We have spoken of prayer as a struggle, even a "warfare to the last breath"[46] in which we come to face parts of ourselves we would rather not see, assimilate losses, and wrestle with God and ourselves for healing. One of the hardest struggles of prayer often comes, however, not when God stands over against us, calling us to painful healing and growth, but when God seems absent.

A friend of mine a year or two ago was suffering through a terrible depression related to a difficult situation at work that was paralleled in his relationship with his daughter at home. He reports that during a period that lasted several months, God felt so entirely absent when he prayed that it seemed God was deliberately withdrawing when he sat down to pray. Even to sit in his chair at all every day was a kind of torture to him. When he was already suffering so much, the temptation to decide that he could no longer pray and to quit was very strong. He was a man well trained by the Abbas and Ammas, however; and he trusted what they had taught him. He continued, "going against himself"[47] until even in God's absence he came to hear God tell him, "For all these years I have held you together and protected you against the childhood wounds you carry in your heart. I want your wholeness, and so I withdraw from you now in order that you seek real healing for those wounds. I stand back, but I am with you." The odd thing, my friend says, is that once he became aware of the meaning of God's absence, sitting in that chair to pray did not get any easier for a long time, but he began to take active steps in the direction of his own healing. Gradually, even with a sense of the absence of God, he realized that now his whole life had become a prayer. At Easter his ordeal was over; the healing of his depression was well begun, and his daily prayer took a new and happy turning.

"Success" in prayer finally has nothing to do with how we feel, not even whether we feel the presence of God. What goes on in our prayer right now is only a small part of the larger prayer of our lifetime. Because prayer is a shared life with God, we must relinquish the idea that our prayer is our own to control as we wish. We must be persistent and brave, willing to trust God enough to believe that whatever form our prayer takes, God is always at work in us in ways we do not know. The woman wrestling with the Psalms and the man wrestling with his depression were terribly tempted to quit their daily practice of prayer. Both felt like failures. One felt that God was hostile; one felt that God was absent. Amma Syncletica said of the monk's temptation to go to another monastery at a time like this,

> "If you find yourself in a monastery do not go to another place, for that will harm you a great deal. Just as the bird who abandons the eggs she was sitting on prevents them from hatching, so the monk or the nun grows cold and their faith dies, when they go from one place to another."[48]

The same is true of us in our prayer. More often than not, it is not in the easy times of our prayer that we grow toward God the most but in the times of chaos, confusion, pain, or even boredom. To quit our prayer then is to let the eggs grow cold.

Because life is always changing, prayer is always changing, too. Gregory of Nyssa was so sure of the truth of this fundamental reality that he described the life of the Christian in eternity itself as a continual and ever-changing growth into the love and life of God.[49]

Prayer is for life. Rather than providing the one who prays with a world apart, it does just the opposite: it carries us into love. Prayer and love remove the boundaries between the "spiritual" and the "everyday." Or, to put it another way, remember Dorotheos's circle. If the ordinary world we live in is the outside of the circle and God is at the center, what joins us to the center is love, and prayer both provides the context and enables love. In the next three chapters, therefore, we will talk about our growth in love and prayer. In chapter 4 we will see how learning to claim our identity in God is necessary to love; chapter 5 will be a discussion of the virtues necessary for love of neighbor; chapter 6 will be about prayer and the love of God.

Chapter 4

"Only Myself and God"

If a life of prayer is also a life of moving toward God and each other in love, the ancient monastics knew that there cannot be love where there is no self to do the loving. The desert Abbas and Ammas were convinced that love of God and the neighbor is the goal as well as the starting point of the Christian life of prayer. As Christians our very lives depend upon our understanding of this truth:

> [Abba Anthony] said, "Our life and our death is with our neighbour. If we gain our brother [or sister], we have gained God, but if we scandalise our brother [or sister], we have sinned against Christ."[1]

Paradoxically, precisely because this love of others and God is the whole of the Christian life, we find this statement at the heart of early monastic teaching:

> Abba Alonius said, "If a [person] does not say in his [or her] heart, in the world there is only myself and God, [that person] will not gain peace."[2]

In this statement Alonius tells us that we cannot even begin to learn to love others without entering first into the Christian task of learning to claim for ourselves a self to do that loving. In this chapter we will see why and how the Abbas and Ammas know this is true.

75

WHY DO I NEED A SELF?

To many modern Christians, loving means that as Jesus gave up his life for others, so Christians must also in their everyday lives give up their very selves for the sake of others.

In some very important senses this is true. All love, even love that is not explicitly Christian, requires self-giving. Parents who love their babies have to be willing to set aside their own need for quiet and undisturbed sleep in order to provide for their needy babies. A person accustomed to working fifteen-hour days, or to spending all his weekend time fishing alone on an isolated lake will need to make some real changes in his life when he marries if he loves his wife and wishes to share a life with her. Teachers who love their students must find time to be available to those students, even if their temperaments urge them to spend ten hours a day locked alone in their studies doing research.

The difficulty comes at the point where we are tempted to think that real Christian love is of such a self-sacrificial nature that Christians ought not have a self at all. Instead they must give themselves away extravagantly for the ones they love, pouring themselves out like water into sand for the sake of those they love and serve. This does not work.

People who go into ministry are particularly vulnerable to this belief that love of others requires giving up the self, and their congregations reinforce them in it. Ministers to a surprising degree object to the idea that they take time each day to rest and be with their families, much less take time to be with God in prayer and study. With so many people around them making demands on their time, they cannot distinguish between being selfish and having legitimate needs. Unfortunately both they and their congregations pay a high price for their confusion as burnout quickly sets in. There is nothing so depressing as a minister two years out of seminary who has already become a hearty-handed empty shell of a person, unable truly to respond to anyone or anything.

Our culture reinforces the belief that real Christian women must give themselves up entirely for the needs and desires of their husbands, families, friends, and churches. Many find themselves unable to justify leaving abusive marriages. Others stay exhausted as they spend all their time at home doing household duties that are meant to prove their selfless love to their families. Still others find themselves continually overcommitting themselves to things they are to do for others, only to find themselves collapsing under their self-inflicted burden, letting others down in crucial situations as they are unable to carry through on their unrealistic promises.

The ancient monastics knew—or, rather, had to learn—that there cannot be love of others, much less love of God, where there is no self to do the loving. They learned that they were not free to ignore the needs of that self or give it away to another person. They could not throw away that self or sell it into bondage or neglect it while still being able to love the people they most sincerely desired to love. They knew this because they knew that this is the very way we are made. Our self is given by God. It is made in the image of God. Its identity is in God, and its primary relationship is to God. This is why Abba Alonius said,

"If a [person] does not say in his [or her] heart, in the world there is only myself and God, he [or she] will not gain peace."

A friend of mine learned the truth of the monastic teaching the hard way. When her two children were small, the family had a difficult life in some ways as she worked to support them as well as caring for them at home. Her older child resented her frequent but unavoidable exhaustion, believing that if she loved him better, she would be less tired and more available to him. Her feelings of guilt told her that his unhappiness was caused by her failure to sacrifice more for him, and so against all reason she tried to "do better." Her renewed efforts, however, did not help. When he was in his late teens, he devised the perfect way to punish her. He bought a motorcycle, and for two years she lived in a state of terror, rage, and further guilt. If he did not kill himself outright, she was sure that he would maim himself for life. In mental agony she went over all she had not done for him over the years, as well as all that she had done wrong. She was eaten up with her failure to be "a better mother," and she felt shamed in front of mothers of children without problems. She begged him to give up the motorcycle, but she bargained to no avail.

Finally, she could take no more. Until this point in her daily prayer she had been asking God to help her be a better mother, but nothing got better. All of a sudden she could see that she must be missing something basic about Christian love. Now she really wrestled with God to discover what that was. Slowly she became able to see how her own identity, her desire to be a good mother was linked with notions about pouring herself out for her children. In anguish and anger she came to see that in her trying to find her identity in her motherhood she had lost not only herself but her son. She discovered that her identity rests only in God, not in being good in any form. Love was not giving herself away for her son, whatever he might think. Emotionally she turned him loose, deciding that killing or maiming himself had to be his decision, not hers. A great weight of depression rolled off her and she began to find peace.

Three weeks later, without any discussion, he sold the motorcycle. He not only found himself safer transportation; in other areas of his life, too, his behavior became far less self-destructive. This does not mean, however, that he became reconciled to his mother. Indeed, now in his twenties, he will not forgive her "abandonment" of him when he could no longer manipulate her. Nevertheless he has finally assumed responsibility for his own life in most areas. Pondering over this whole process in her prayer over many months, his mother finally came to understand how her conviction that she should pour herself out for her son actually had prevented her from seeing his real needs. He needed her to stand over against him and say, "Because I love you, I will not allow you to tell me whether I am valuable as a person; only God can do that. Because I love you, you must assume responsibility for your own life, even if it makes you hate me."

In early monastic terms, to try to live without a self is a passion. The distortion of who we are that comes of such an attempt is the source of many wounds to ourselves and to others. These wounds prevent us from loving by keeping us from being able realistically to see and react to each other, the world, and God.

These wounds are compounded by many often interrelated permutations of failing to claim our identity in God. Although it would be profitable to spend a little time examining several more, we will look at three: feeling that the value of our self is determined by others' approval or liking of us, blaming others for our own lack of control, and perfectionism.[3]

THE NEED FOR APPROVAL

In my friend's wrestling to understand why her self-sacrificial love of her son was not helping him, she came to see that her own desire to be a good mother was itself causing harm. She did not really believe she could be that good mother unless he believed that she was. Without his approval of her, she felt like a failure as a human being. The ability or inability to lay hold of this identity apart from other people's reaction to us affects us at every point in our lives together. At a private level men and women find themselves unable to leave marriages that are destroying their spouses, themselves, and their children out of anxiety that they will somehow lose themselves if others see them as "bad people." Often we simply feel powerless if we find that we have lost someone else's good opinion. Publicly our need for approval may keep us from speaking the truth to each other or otherwise acting on our convictions. The civil rights movement could never have taken place without men and women willing to stand against the very laws of the land and be willing to be told that they were bad people for so standing. Our churches suffer appallingly from ministers so paralyzed by a need for approval that they have become unable to stand over against their congregations, to be moral leaders of their people.

Monastics, who understood that their relationships to others were closely linked to their relationship to God, were terribly vulnerable to slipping into a belief that their own worth came from the good or bad opinion of others. A fundamental part of their training was aimed at learning that the monastic's identity is not constituted by other people's approval or diminished by other people's insults or lack of recognition. The monastic needed to realize that Christian identity lies in God, not in whether others admired their ascetic discipline, wisdom, or goodness or were offended by their lack of conformity to other people's expectations.

To this end the Abbas and Ammas repeatedly told their disciples to regard themselves simply as dead with respect to other people's opinion:

> A brother came to see Abba Macarius the Egyptian, and said to him, "Abba, give me a word, that I may be saved." So the old man said, "Go to the cemetery and abuse the dead." The brother went there, abused them and threw stones at them; then he returned and told the old man about it. The latter said to him "Didn't they say anything to you?" He replied, "No." The old man said, "Go back tomorrow and praise them." So the brother went away and praised them, calling them, "Apostles, saints, and righteous men." He returned to the old man and said to

him, "I have complimented them." And the old man said to him, "Did they not answer you?" The brother said no. The old man said to him, "You know how you insulted them and they did not reply, and how you praised them and they did not speak; so you too if you wish to be saved must do the same and become a dead man. Like the dead, take no account of either the scorn of [human beings] or their praises, and you can be saved."[4]

The clear implication in Macarius's suggestion is that unless we are able to know that our ultimate identity is not linked to other people's evaluation of us, we will be lost.

PERFECTIONISM

Perfectionism is another threat to self. While in our need for approval we grant others the right to give or withhold value to ourselves, the passion of perfectionism stems from believing that we must earn our self because our real value comes not from God but from what we do and how we do it. One manifestation of perfectionism in the desert was the compulsion beginners often felt to go beyond the advice of the Abbas or Ammas on frequency of prayer. Being unable to trust that their value to God did not come at least partly from their own efforts to pray, they would wake up several times a night to pray when they ought to have been sleeping. Consequently they would quickly burn out and so leave monastic life altogether. Often a perfectionistic monk would forget that the point of ascetical disciplines was the increase of love rather than earning salvation. As a result he or she would be tempted to indulge in ever more stringent and actually self-defeating practices.

One of the Fathers telling about the Cells, said there was once a hard-working old man there who wore a mat [made out of scratchy rope in place of clothes]. He went to find Abba Ammonas, who, when he saw him wearing the mat, said to him, "This is no use to you."

The old man, however, was not even able to hear what Ammonas was saying to him about his perfectionism, and he went on to compound the matter by questioning him further about how to increase his asceticism.

"Three thoughts occupy me, either, should I wander in the deserts, or should I go to a foreign land where no-one knows me, or should I shut myself up in a cell without opening the door to anyone, eating only every second day." Abba Ammonas replied, "It is not right for you to do any of these three things. Rather, sit in your cell and eat a little every day, keeping the world of the publican always in your heart, and you may be saved."[5]

What does the passion of perfectionism look like in modern dress? It comes in an enormous number of guises. Believing that if we prayed more, loved more or better, tried harder to keep our commitments, no matter how soul destroying, worked harder, we would be "better" people is perfectionism. Being judgmental about people who do not have to work as hard as we is perfectionism. Procrastination or inability to complete projects for fear of failure is a form of perfectionism. Inability to make changes in our lives unless they are radical and sweeping often comes from a kind of all-or-nothing thinking that is perfectionistic. In one of its most painful and pervasive forms, perfectionism can keep us in a constant state of feeling guilty over imagined failures in all areas of our lives. In all its forms perfectionism is a passion that causes us to feel that our right to our very life is tied up in whether we succeed at whatever it is that is important to us. This desperation in turn prevents us from being able truly to turn our love to other people.

NAMING MYSELF AS VICTIM

Often closely related to the preceding difficulties we encounter as we fail to find our identity in God is the problem of identifying ourselves as victims of the people we mean to love and serve. This was also a monastic problem.[6] We can return here to a story we looked at earlier.

A brother was restless in the community and often moved to anger. So he said: "I will go, and live somewhere by myself. And since I shall be able to talk or listen to no one, I shall be tranquil, and my passionate anger will cease." He went out and lived alone in a cave. But one day he filled his jug with water and put it on the ground. It happened suddenly to fall over. He filled it again, and again it fell. And this happened a third time. And in a rage he snatched up the jug and broke it. Returning to his right mind, he knew that the demon of anger had mocked him, and he said: . . . "I will return to the community. Wherever you live, you need effort and patience and above all God's help."

Repeatedly the Abbas and Ammas teach their disciples to look for ways they themselves are responsible for their own mistakes and failings, so that, taking responsibility for those messes, they may make changes in their lives. Perfectionism is characterized in all its varieties by overtly or subtly blaming other people and even God for our inability to be who we want to be. Suffering from this passion, if we identify ourselves as victim, or place most of the blame for our condition outside ourselves, we also take away from ourselves our own ability to affect what happens to us. In its overt forms our trapping of ourselves in a victim mentality is obvious: "If I had never married you, I would have been a doctor," or "I cannot take this class; it will upset my husband," or "The people at church would think I am an irresponsible bum if I quit this job."

In its less obvious forms, however, habitually placing the blame outside ourselves for our own inability to claim our identity can be even more devastating but harder to see because it so often goes under the guise of Christian love. "I will have to skip my day off to go to the hospital and visit Mrs. Smith; she gets her feelings hurt so easily," a minister will say. A lover or spouse struggling with a soul-destroying relationship says, "I know that the person I am in this relationship violates everything I want to be and believe I ought to be. He needs me, though; if I left him, it would kill him." A teacher, continually setting aside her own research to talk to a chronically troubled student who always has an emergency to discuss might say, "My student has had such a bad life, and he has no one else to pay attention to him; how can I turn him away?" Soon, where they intended to act out of love, they are filled with anger and guilt.

Love, at least in the beginning, did motivate each of these people, but that is not the whole of it. Each wants to believe that loving leaves no option except to give up any claims for the needs of self at all. They believe that their ability to begin to claim themselves depends upon the people they serve recognizing their servers' needs and giving them permission to care for their own needs. They are suffering from a passion; they do not see that this will not happen by itself. They have chosen to give themselves away.

They will have to choose to work at claiming back the self that must be there if there is to be real and generous love.

BEGINNING TO CLAIM OUR SELVES IN GOD

Saying "In the world there is only myself and God" is one thing. Trying to live it out is another. How do we do it when the world of people, jobs, and organizations tells us daily "You belong to me"? When our own deepest feelings, habits, and patterns of behavior work against us, is it even possible?

It is true that the task is hard. We learned what it means to claim a self early and well from a hodgepodge of places: what the authority figures in our lives—parents and grandparents and Sunday school teachers—told us and modeled for us; things we heard from other children; things we worked out ourselves about what God must be like and what God requires of us. Some of what we learned is true to the gospel and gives us life. Much of it relating to the evils of "selfishness" or "self-centeredness" is not true to the gospel at all and it hurts us. Often we recognize the parts of what we believe that cause us great pain, and we are able to see how they are a betrayal of the gospel. Our very inability to escape the internal power of these Christian childhood "truths" convinces us that while they may be true for no one else, they must be true for us. Reading a few books and coming to an intellectual understanding of the reality of our situation cannot deliver us from our wounds.

Our difficulties are compounded when we believe that somehow we ought simply to decide to claim our identity in God and then do it. Having made an intellectual decision, we expect that our feelings as well as our patterns of thought and behavior ought to conform overnight to that decision. When we find they have not, we become discouraged and give up. We lacerate ourselves with guilt and hopelessness.

We have fallen once more into a confusion between what is essentially a goal of the Christian life and its starting point. The monastics assume that in the Christian life there is nearly always a real gap between our head learning and our heart learning. In chapter 2 we noted that while the Abbas and Ammas believed that love of God and neighbor was the whole point of the Christian life, they were equally convinced that learning to love in this way was the work of a whole lifetime.

In the same way, if we already have to have claimed our identity in God before we can begin to be Christians, no one will be Christian. It is an ongoing part of our whole life's work. Acknowledging our need to find our existence in God belongs to the beginning, the middle, and the end of the Christian life. Rather than becoming demoralized at how great the task seems, we need to know that being increasingly able to claim our identity in God and live out of it is a fundamental part of growth in the Christian life.

We must work at giving up heroic images of instant transformation, accepting instead that even if we finally are aiming at a major decision about our lives in terms of career or marriage or parenting, we still prepare for the larger decisions by learning to claim our identity a little at a time on a daily basis. The story in the preceding chapter about the brother who was told to clear his plot of land by just working each day on the space he took up when he lay down for his nap is as applicable here as it was on the subject of prayer.

We start by becoming convinced of the necessity of having a self; we go on to choose to have a self, and then we try to act upon that choice as best we can. It is important to remember, however, that the whole process is not a matter of our own effort, like learning to tie shoes. The author of the *Macarian Homilies* promises his attentive listener that if one practices, difficult as that may be, God will finally give him or her such grace that the inner self will be transformed.

> And thus, the things he [or she] now does with effort of a reluctant heart, he [or she] may perform one day willingly, accustoming himself [or herself] always to the good and remembering the Lord and waiting for [God] always in great love.[7]

In this process we have the ongoing, day-to-day help of the Holy Spirit, comforting us, pushing us, giving us insight in our prayer and through other people and otherwise empowering us to do and be what may seem to us right now impossibly far off.

PRAYING FOR OURSELVES

What do we need to do, then, to begin to find our identity in God?

> A brother said to Abba Anthony, "Pray for me," The old man said to him, "I will have no mercy upon you, nor will God have any, if you yourself do not make an effort and if you do not pray to God."[8]

God does not force the fact of our true identity upon us. We must "make an effort" to seek it and ask for it. We begin this process of claiming our identity in God by praying for ourselves.

Praying for ourselves is often not easy for people having trouble claiming a self. As we discussed in chapter 3, this can be particularly true for people who are not accustomed to thinking of themselves as having a right to take the time for it. Others believe that it is selfish to pray for oneself in the face of the needs of the people around them as well as the larger world's need. But beginners are not the only ones to struggle with prayer for themselves. It is not unusual even for those who have had a long experience of daily prayer to endure periods when it is extremely hard to pray for themselves. It is not for nothing that this conversation took place between Agathon and his disciples.

> The brethren . . . asked him, "Among all good works, which is the virtue which requires the most effort?" He answered, "Forgive me, but I think there is no labor greater than that of prayer to God. For every time a [person] wants to pray, his enemies, the demons, want to prevent him, for they know that it is only by turning him from prayer that they can hinder his journey. Whatever good work a [person] undertakes, if [that person] perseveres in it, [that person] will attain rest. But prayer is warfare to the last breath.[9]

The monastic teachers were firm. Difficult as it may be, we still must pray for ourselves.

Praying for ourselves has many facets. At its simplest, if we are able to see the areas in ourselves where we specifically need God's grace, it is helpful to ask God directly. This does not necessarily mean making long speeches to God on our own behalf. Here we can heed Macarius's advice when asked "how should one pray?"

> "There is no need at all to make long discourses; it is enough to stretch out one's hand and say, 'Lord as you will, and as you know, have mercy.' And if the conflict grows fiercer say, 'Lord, help!' [God] knows very well what we need and [God] shows us [God's] mercy."[10]

Or we can ask, "Help me to resist giving myself away when I refuse to acknowledge my own need for free time, and give me courage to claim it."

If we are still not convinced that we need or are entitled to a self, or if we are convinced that we do, but claiming that self does not seem all that straightforward, our prayer will not be so simple. Perhaps more often than not we cannot even see what we need. When this is the case, praying Scripture is invaluable.

SCRIPTURE

Scripture is God's special gift to God's people, and it is intended to be a gift of life. If we pray Scripture daily with open hearts, it will teach us about having a self in God. As we heard in the last chapter, Abba Poemen, who had great faith in the slow but steady healing power of Scripture, once said,

> "The nature of water is soft, that of stone is hard; but if a bottle is hung above the stone, allowing the water to fall drop by drop, it wears away the stone. So it is with the word of God; it is soft and our heart is hard, but the [person] who hears the word of God often opens his [or her] heart to the fear of God."[11]

It was a fundamental conviction of the early monastics that the very hearing and repeating of the words and images of Scripture over a long time has a powerful ability to form and shape our understanding as Christians.

Our encounter with Scripture cannot be simply a passive process, however. We must decide to listen for it to speak freeing and illuminating words to us. To this end we begin our prayer by asking God for help both in hearing and in believing that Scripture is meant to be a source of life to us, and not destruction. Then we do the work of reading attentively and listening actively to hear in our hearts as well as our heads what God tells us through Scripture about claiming our identity in God. Just as important, as we later in the day think about what we have read, we must ask persistently, "What does this passage tell me about my identity in God?"

Scripture itself offers many metaphors to encourage our persistence. Jacob wrestled all night with an angel to obtain God's blessing, and through his persistence God blessed him.[12] Luke's

Gospel says that for the very purpose of encouraging his hearers "to pray continually and never lose heart," Jesus told the story of the widow who argued with the corrupt judge to see justice done her until he finally saw her vindicated.[13] Repeatedly, Jesus is portrayed in the Gospels as healing variously crippled men and women who simply with their whole hearts desired and persisted in seeking healing. As we persist in our serious struggle with Scripture and with God to claim our identities in God, we know that God has promised we will finally claim them. Then we, with Arsenius, will find it true that,

"if we seek God, [God] will show [God's self] to us, and if we keep [God], [God] will remain close to us."[14]

What does Scripture say about finding our selves in God? The stories of creation do not stand at the beginning of the Bible in order to tell us what came first chronologically in human history. They are there to tell every hearer of Scripture, "You are valuable to God in a special way. You are the image of God; God made you to belong to God. God loves and wants you to be God's own friend;[15] for this you must have a self to choose God in return. It is a good thing to be a human being from God's point of view; you cannot possibly have to give up what God gave you in the first place to be who God wants you to be. God loves you so much that your name is written in the palm of God's hand.[16]

This is the starting point of Jesus' own teaching. The story of the rich fool illustrates that unless we claim this self everything else is lost. His energies only went into amassing wealth as he said to himself, " 'My soul, you have plenty of good things laid by for many years to come; take things easy, eat, drink, have a good time.' But God said to him, 'Fool! This very night the demand will be made for your soul; and this hoard of yours, whose will it be then?' "[17]

The need to not have the self determined by other people's expectations was crucial to Jesus' own behavior. Most fundamental, of course, was Jesus' refusal to be the kind of military Davidic messiah everybody was expecting. On a day-to-day level we meet Jesus in the Gospels refusing to accept the validity of his own family's desire for him to conform to their expectations that he ought to give up his ministry, go home with them, and stop acting like a crazy person.[18] Jesus did not worry about the indecency of himself as a teacher of the Jewish law eating with sinners. He had his own understanding of what it meant to be a teacher. Jesus' Sabbath healing of the man with the withered hand[19] and his socially rude acceptance in Simon's house of the perfume of the long-haired woman who wept on his feet[20] are two stories illustrating Jesus' teaching from his behavior.

Jesus did not tell people to accept their roles in life and be happy with the status quo. The necessity of reclaiming this self from the grip of social, religious, and cultural expectations was a fundamental part of Jesus' teaching. He called others to turn their backs on the need to be "good" and do what was expected and approved in their world. He preached a radical message:

> "Do not suppose that I have come to bring peace to the earth: it is not peace I have come to bring, but a sword. For I have come to set son against father, daughter against mother, daughter-in-law against mother-in-law; a person's enemies will be the members of his own household."[21]

Thus he congratulated Mary for talking to him, and he chided Martha for worrying over whether Mary was doing what was expected of her socially when Jesus came to dinner.[22] We hear Jesus repeatedly call other people to leave behind what keeps them from themselves to claim their identities in God. We know of many direct invitations Jesus issued: to the individual apostles; to the Samaritan woman he met at the well; to Zacchaeus to come out of the tree to entertain Jesus; to various scribes and Pharisees who chose to be Jesus' enemies.

Jesus never suggests that human beings' value comes from all that they do right, nor that they become less valuable if they are not perfect. Indeed, just the opposite is true. One of the saddest stories in the Gospels is that of the rich young ruler.[23] He could not give up his possessions, it is true; just as serious, however, was his inability to give up his belief that it was precisely by "keeping the law" perfectly that he had become who he was. The story of the two brothers in the parable of the prodigal son is a good example of Jesus' refusal to value people according to their goodness.[24] The father in the story did not value the "good" son who stayed home and worked any more than he loved and valued the "bad" son who went away.

Even to us who do not abandon everything to follow Jesus, Jesus calls through Scripture to claim our identity in God. But he warns us: That claim always involves having to leave behind an old image of the self that belongs instead to family or to a congregation or boss or more general social obligations. Leaving the old image, the old self is going to hurt sometimes so much it feels like death.

"If anyone wants to be a follower of mine, let him [or her] renounce his [or her] life and follow me. Anyone who wants to save his [or her] life will lose it; but anyone who loses his [or her] life for my sake, will save it."[25]

Courage, as well as persistence, is necessary for this task. The Old Testament is full of stories of the courage God's people needed in order to answer the call to claim their true identities in God. In Genesis we see seventy-five-year-old Abraham responding immediately to God's summons and promise: "Leave your country, your kindred and your father's house for a country which I shall show you; and I shall make you a great nation."[26] In Exodus we meet Moses, having fled Egypt as a murderer, finding the courage to answer God's call to go and confront Pharaoh himself on behalf of the Israelites.[27] In the books of the prophets, too, we often hear the pain of the prophets who are asked by their God to lose their lives in order to gain them: to choose between satisfying their country's expectations of them and claiming their identities in God by speaking the truth.

Abba Poemen used the analogy of the wearing away of rock by dripping water to describe the steady power of Scripture to shape our hearts. Abba Mathois said,

"I want to find some easy but continual work, rather than a heavy work that is quickly finished."[28]

For us, praying Scripture is just such work as we seek what it means to find ourselves in God.

PRAYER AND SELF-UNDERSTANDING

Seeing that we need a self in God, and hearing deeply how Scripture supports and encourages us to claim that self, are not the whole of our prayer. We will not make progress in claiming that identity unless we are able to look within ourselves and see how our own actions, attitudes, memories, and habits work against our desire for God. This is what Abba Poemen meant when he said,

"Not understanding what has happened prevents us from going on to something better."[29]

Introspection is thus a very important part of the process of finding our identity.

Looking for the places God has worked and is now working within us is part of the task of introspection. We mull over our own histories and find in them the times and places where by God's grace our true selves have been enabled to make decisions: in our choice of a career; in our handling of our children; in our relationship with friends. In this case the practice of introspection becomes the singing of a kind of love song of gratitude and joy to God for God's good gifts.[30]

Introspection can be excruciating. This is another reason Abba Agathon says that "prayer is warfare to the last breath."[31] A friend of mine recalled one morning praying through Psalm 139, the great psalm that acknowledges that God "searches me and knows me" in the most intimate detail and has done so even from before birth. When he concluded the psalm he asked God to share with him God's own knowledge of him. As soon as the words were out of his mouth, however, he told me, he was filled with fear and dread. He did not want God's knowledge of himself. How could he bear to know some of those things? It was a long time before he was able to pray that prayer again.

How do we find these self-destructive patterns when looking within ourselves for them? Some we know already, if we are willing to admit it to ourselves. Others are easy to spot if we are honest and we really want to find them. To this end Evagrius recommended becoming close enough observers of ourselves to keep track of our states of mind and behavior throughout the day. In fact he advises his monks to keep a journal for this purpose.[32]

Part of the very nature of a passion, however, is its capacity to blind. Where there is a passion there is usually some form of self-deception, what Dorotheos calls "lying in our imagination." The alcoholic characteristically explains away her drinking to herself. The person suffering from avarice will not spend money on heating the house even when it is below zero because she is saving for an emergency—an emergency that can never, in fact, be worse than the one she is already in. In the same way the person struggling to claim an identity in God is likely to explain away the ways she or he colludes in giving away that identity. A minister who cannot face the disapproval of his congregation will tell himself, "Love requires me to give up my day off, which my family is looking forward to, to visit Mrs. Jones in the hospital."

Even where there is no real self-deception, however, we often cannot see what it is in ourselves that contributes to our difficulties. The early monastics had their Abbas, Ammas, and fellows to help them see and understand their passions. We all need help, too. Some of it we can get by listening to and considering seriously within the context of our prayer the truth of what even hostile people around us say to us: "You're always working"; "Don't take yourself so seriously"; "You're always blaming me." Christian friends that we trust to know us, share our values, and speak the truth as they understand it are even more valuable.

Some of the passions that keep us from claiming ourselves and God sometimes seem unreachable, even with the help of sincere introspection and the conversation of friends. The roots of these passions are too far back in the past, in events and memories that wound us and bind us. In these cases psychologists, pastoral counselors, or psychiatrists can be of amazing help. Perhaps surprisingly, in their indirect ways of helping us understand ourselves, they even often function very similarly to the ancient teachers. They can help us find the very places in ourselves we need to submit to God's healing, but they also can help us see how we can actually act to aid in this healing and claiming of our identity.

MAKING THE EFFORT TO ACT CONSISTENTLY WITH OUR PRAYER

If you recall, when Anthony refused to pray for the man who asked him, he did so saying,

"I will have no mercy upon you, and neither will God have any, if you yourself do not make an effort and if you do not pray to God."[33]

We have already seen how important it is to want to find our identities in God. Wishing is the beginning of hope. It can be very painful and difficult to do, but hope often needs to be exercised even against our feelings to become a reality. As an exercise of hope, we can begin pondering actively and imaginatively throughout the day what it really means concretely to have our identities in God.

Part of the work of our prayer is to begin consciously in other ways as well to bring our prayer and our lives into harmony with one another. That our life and our prayer must be all of a piece was a basic principle of early monastic life. As we heard in the last chapter, Moses, the great black Abba from the Sudan, expressed this very simply.

> If a [person's] deeds are not in harmony with his [or her] prayer, [that person] labors in vain. The brother said, "What is this harmony between practice and prayer?" The old man said, "We should no longer do those things against which we pray."[34]

Moses could just as well have added, "and we should do those things that are in harmony with the things for which we pray." Doing or avoiding these things that are in harmony with, that support and complete our prayer constitutes "making an effort" so that our prayer may bear fruit in our lives.

What sorts of things need to be lined up with our prayer? As part of our daily work we need resolutely to decide that we will not internally collude in the destruction of our own identity in God. We must give up calling ourselves names or otherwise punishing ourselves where we find ourselves inadequate in any area of our lives. Few of us respond well to bullying. Most of us are only demoralized by it, the exact opposite of what we are asking God for in our prayer when we seek to find ourselves.[35]

We can also decide that rather than collapsing when we are confronted with some of the things that hurt us, we practice using them to learn new attitudes. As we have seen, the need for others' approval was always a major temptation for beginning monks. Their steadfast advice was to seek out insults:

> Abba Isaiah said, "Nothing is so useful to the beginner as insults. The beginner who bears insults is like a tree that is watered every day."[36]

Few of us would really want to seek out insults, but many people have found it useful to take the occasion of a wounding remark that they are inclined to use to reinforce their own sense of inadequacy to practice fighting internally for their own identity instead. Surprisingly, when one is willing to take this risk, the occasion that begins in pain can end in a sense of power to define one's own identity.

We need also to try to give up colluding in external ways in the destruction of our identity and integrity in God. This is much harder and more painful. It may involve ending a job that is stealing our soul. Sometimes it entails stopping another person's abusive control of us. This can mean ending a relationship or drastically changing its shape.

The need to take such drastic action was what drove the early monastics to the desert in the first place. Even in the desert, however, monks had to continue to make such decisions, as we see in the following story. To understand the story, remember that in the Egyptian desert the obedience and loyalty a disciple owed an Abba or Amma were nearly absolute:

> A brother questioned Abba Poemen, saying, "I am losing my soul through living near my abba; should I go on living with him?" The old man knew that he was finding this harmful and he was surprised that he even asked if he should stay there. So he said to him, "Stay if you want to." The brother left him and stayed on there. He came back again and said, "I am losing my soul." But the old man did not tell him to leave. He came a third time and said, "I really cannot stay there any longer." Then Abba Poemen said, "Now you are saving yourself; go away and do not stay with him any longer," and he added, "When someone sees that he [or she] is in danger of losing his [or her] soul, he [or she] does not need to ask advice."[37]

What was putting the disciple's very self in jeopardy is irrelevant to the story. Perhaps the Abba was too lenient and thus permitted the disciple to fritter away his life gossiping. Perhaps he was so judgmental that the disciple was consumed with anxiety and despair. What is relevant is the lesson of the story: Care for the self takes priority even over obedience to the Abba.

More often, however, these changes are not so earthshaking. Praying for courage and steadiness, we can begin, against our own feelings, to make small decisions for ourselves that support our identity. If it is what we need to do, we can say no when asked to help out at church when we need time to ourselves, even though it makes us feel guilty. We can work at building a discipline of prayer, even though we feel we should be doing something useful. When we are abused in minor ways we can refuse to accept the abuse as deserved. Against our own perfectionism we can deliberately practice letting other people do what we have always done if we wanted it done "right."

THE GOAL IS LOVE

An old friend of mine has been married close to thirty years. Most of this time she had a painful relationship with her mother-in-law, who habitually went out of her way to tell my friend about what a terrible wife and mother she was. Several years ago my friend decided to handle the pain, humiliation, and anger of it by avoiding the older woman; she did not willingly visit, and when she did, she did not let herself be engaged emotionally in conversation. Meanwhile her mother-in-law continued to be verbally abusive whenever she had the chance.

Recently my friend's father-in-law died, and her husband's mother came for her first visit in years. The abuse began again right on schedule. This time was different, however. In a terribly painful extended conversation my friend told her mother-in-law that she would not let her address her in the same way anymore and why. After the initial shock of having another person stand up to her, the older woman came to see what she had been doing, and the price in terms of her own loneliness that she had been paying. Now the relationship of the two women is different. My friend is not only no longer subject to the same abuse, she is able to love her mother-in-law. For the first time she can to be present to her and do things for her mother-in-law, who now needs and appreciates her very much.

When we seek our identity in God, we are not finally searching for a healthy, self-confident self, a fully realized self, or even a good character. Paradoxically, what follows from learning to say, "In the world there is only myself and God," is the deep knowledge that the self does not exist for itself alone.

The conclusion of Alonius's saying is that we should be seeking to "gain peace." Surely he means more than "peace of mind," resting tranquilly in God's hands while the anguish of everyday life passes by. About the monastic life Abba Poemen said,

"Even if [we] were to make a new heaven and a new earth, [we] could not live free from care."[38]

Peace does not cut us off from others, nor is it even dependent upon freedom from a certain amount of external chaos. Another story of Poemen illustrates this well:

Abba Poemen's brothers said to him, "Let us leave this place, for the monasteries here worry us and we are losing our souls; even the little children who cry do not let us have interior peace." Abba Poemen said to them, "Is it because of the voices of angels that you wish to go away from here?"[39]

Peace is a deep disposition of the heart. It is an ability to let go of the need to be right, an ability based on the knowledge that our rightness or wrongness in any issue is totally irrelevant to God's love for us or for our neighbor. The peace that comes with claiming our self in God is the foundation of our ability to love others in the most humble places and everyday ways. Once more Poemen speaks a word:

A brother going to market asked Abba Poemen, "How do you advise me to behave?" The old man said to him, "Make friends with anyone who tries to bully you and sell your produce in peace."[40]

Peace is finally God's gift to us, but it is a gift to be shared for the reconciliation of the world.

Chapter 5

"Our Life and Death Is with Our Neighbor"

*A*bba Anthony said,

> "Our life and our death is with our neighbour. If we gain our brother [or sister] we have gained God, but if we scandalise our brother [or sister], we have sinned against Christ."[1]

The fulfillment of our deepest purposes and our profoundest longings for God can never be separated from our love of God's own images among whom we live. We find ourselves in God not for a self-fulfillment that will make us independent from the need for other people but in order to love.

Recall once more the diagram of reality that Dorotheos drew. It was a circle, representing the world, with lines, standing for human lives, drawn from the outside of the circle to the center point, which is God. By means of this diagram Dorotheos demonstrated to his monks the way in which love of God and neighbor are interconnected: If human lives come to God by moving along the radii of the circle, it is clear that no one can make this journey to God without drawing closer to the neighbor at the same time.

Dorotheos's diagram assumes that this model of love is one of deep mutuality. In his circle there is no way that one line or one life can be more significant than another. No single line gains its place in the circle by its dominance over any other. Because we are so little accustomed to living according to models of mutuality even in our Christian communities, however, growth in love is not automatic. According to the monastics, learning the ways of love is a matter of unlearning deep patterns of domination and submission and passivity and violence that we, in our not-always-Christian culture, have come to believe are just the way things are or perhaps even the way God wants things to be. The Christian virtues the monastic teachers hold out to us stand in real opposition to competitiveness, rugged individualism, envy, the kind of pride that will not admit fault to another person, and the need to get even for injuries.

This is why Anthony also said,

"Whoever hammers a lump of iron, first decides what he is going to make of it, a scythe, a sword, or an axe. Even so we ought to make up our minds what kind of virtue we want to forge or we labor in vain."[2]

In order to grow in love, Christians must make choices about what kinds of patterns of love they want to grow into. An examination of these patterns, which the monastics call the virtues, and how we live into them is the subject of this chapter.

As we enter into our topic, however, we must paraphrase the question the lawyer asked Jesus. "Who is my neighbor with whom I am trying to grow in love?" The ancient monastics, of course, believed the whole world to be their neighbors. Anthony speaks in moving terms about God's final gathering together and restoring of all people to unity and love.[3] Wherever we meet them in the ancient world—whether advising emperors,[4] talking to pagan priests,[5] exercising pastoral care of thieves, or caring for unwed pregnant peasant girls[6]—we find them offering compassion, forgiveness, healing, charity, advice, and other help to people very different from themselves. The monks were convinced, however, that the first help they could give toward the reconciliation of the world was learning to live in and model love in their own communities. At the same time they did not believe that they would be able to act in love toward those outside their own communities if they did not first begin to love one another. For this reason, in the following pages the emphasis tends to be on the virtues needed for growing in love in the intimate Christian communities of friendship, marriage, family, and church.

THE PROCESS OF GROWTH

According to the monastic teachers, wanting to love does not make us loving people. Such a desire may very well turn us around and set us on a different course in life, making us able to understand what we could not see before. It may even fill our hearts with affection for the people around us for a good while after.

Love, however, is more than simply warm feelings toward others. It is a disposition that involves whole patterns and habits of acting, seeing, and listening to other people on a day-to-day basis.[7] For the early monastics taking on these concrete, particular, daily patterns and habits of love, which they called the virtues, is a fundamental part of learning how to love.

This is not a fast process. Our ancestors were convinced that, for whatever reason, God does not uproot the entire pattern of our thoughts, feelings, and behavior all at once. Nor do we simply decide that from now on we will be fully loving. Whether inflicted upon us by others as children or by ourselves, the wounds to our ability to love cannot be healed all at once. God has given us the job of learning how to love God and each other as our lifetime work.

What about people who claim to have had their whole lives turned around all at once by a single conversion experience? In fact, no one would deny that alcoholics, drug addicts, and others in the grip of addictive behavior most certainly do sometimes find themselves freed of their destructive addictions in a single moment. These events are surely to be celebrated as among the good gifts of our healing God. Nevertheless the Abbas and Ammas give us two warnings. First, we must never fall into the trap of believing that mastery of one pattern of behavior, even one so serious as alcoholism, will make us into loving people. Even under the influence of God's healing grace, a person who is systematically inconsiderate of others does not automatically become considerate. Second, if we fall into the trap of thinking that such instant healing is God's most common, everyday way of working with us, we put ourselves under the impossible and unnecessary burden of expecting that if we could only ask in the right way or do the right thing, God would also make us able to forgive, free us from destructive anger, or make us sensitive to the needs of the people around us.

As we have already seen in both chapter 3, on prayer, and chapter 4, on claiming our identity in God, we really need to believe in and understand that not only is our growth in these areas nearly always slow, this gradual process is the way God chooses to work with us.

> A brother lived in the Cells and in his solitude he was troubled. He went to tell Abba Theodore of Pherme about it. The old man said to him, "Go, be more humble in your aspirations, place yourself under obedience and live with others." Later, he came back to the old man and said, "I do not find any peace with others." The old man said to him, "If you are not at peace either alone or with others, why have you become a monk? Is it not to suffer trials? Tell me how many years you have worn the habit?" He replied, "For eight years." Then the old man said to him, "I have worn the habit seventy years and on no day have I found peace. Do you expect to obtain peace in eight years?" At these words the brother went away strengthened.[8]

Have we not become Christians? The fact of this slowness ought not be discouraging. It is good news. It tells us to lay aside our perfectionism and our perpetual guilt about all we have not done and still cannot do.

THE PATTERNS OF LOVE

To my knowledge no one in the desert tried to make a systematic list of the virtues in the same way Evagrius made a list of the passions.[9] There was no reason they should have. The virtues, after all, are not laws that we follow but interrelated ways of being, feeling, seeing, acting, and reacting in the world that make love and its expressions possible. Thus we are not surprised to find that in the desert some teachers recommended that the monk work on acquiring many virtues simultaneously.[10] Others sought a single master virtue that included all the rest,[11] like Theodore of Pherme, who said,

"There is no other virtue than that of not being scornful."[12]

In these pages we cannot discuss all the monastic virtues, and so I have tried to bring forward those which I believe are most helpful to the modern Christian who is trying to learn the ways of love. Even so, our monastic teachers believed that the virtues, like the passions, are intimately interrelated. Just as one never suffers from only one passion, one cannot possess only one virtue. This is why you will notice that talk of the patterns of one virtue nearly always overlaps with that of another: Nonjudgmentalism is impossible without humility; humility is not possible without consultation; consultation depends upon forgiveness; forgiveness is never independent of discernment. Human ways of being are never tidy, and this is only as it should be.

PRAYER

Prayer is the first of all the virtues the monastics would teach us. The brothers once asked Abba Agathon,

"Amongst all good works, which is the virtue which requires the greatest effort?" He answered, "Forgive me, but I think there is no labour greater than that of prayer to God."[13]

Perhaps it seems strange to think of prayer as a virtue. Remember, however, that a virtue in monastic terms is a whole way of being, of seeing, feeling, and thinking, as well as acting. As we will see, for the monastics the work of prayer is never separated from growth in the patterns of love. Prayer is the place where in a special way we make ourselves vulnerable to God's grace, which helps us understand the virtues, choose them for ourselves, think them through, mull over what in us stands in their way, and gives us the courage to try to live them out in concrete ways. As we have seen already, the practice of prayer is itself a way of being.

Prayer, no matter how private and individual in one sense, is the fundamental foundation of life together within the people of God. When we listen to the stories of the Ammas and Abbas, we find our teachers continually asking for one another's prayers, as well as praying for one another and for those outside their communities. The desert all day long, and all night, too, was crisscrossed with continual prayer for one another's safety, support, healing, forgiveness, encouragement, understanding, and conversion. The continual movement of prayer in our communities is fundamental to the growth of our lives in love of one another and the world God entrusts to us.

HUMILITY

Humility is the next most basic of all the monastic virtues, the distinguishing mark of the Christian.

> When Abba Macarius was returning from the marsh to his cell one day carrying some palm-leaves, he met the devil on the road with a scythe. The latter struck at him as much as he pleased, but in vain, and he said to him, "What is your power, Macarius, that makes me powerless against you? All that you do, I do, too; you fast, so do I; you keep vigil; and I do not sleep at all; in one thing only do you beat me." Abba Macarius asked what that was. He said, "Your humility. Because of that I can do nothing against you."[14]

What is humility? In some important respects it is the master virtue that includes all the others.[15] It is not a matter of deliberately cultivating low self-esteem and a doormat mentality, as we might think. Rather, for the monastic teachers being humble meant knowing that we are all beloved children of God, that the worth of each person comes not from ourselves but from God. Because this is true, the humble man or woman knows that it is not part of any Christian's job to judge or be scornful of other people.

A humble person is one who is, on the one hand, able to accept responsibility toward others for what he does wrong without feeling humiliated by it, and, on the other, to accept praise or thanks without feeling particularly embarrassed or lording it over others because of his or her accomplishments.

Likewise, because a humble person is realistic about all human vulnerabilities, she is not unduly shocked or disillusioned when other human beings make even terrible mistakes. When it comes to living together, humility is the opposite of perfectionism. It gives up unrealistic expectations of how things ought to be for a clear vision of what human life is really like. In turn, this enables its possessors to see and thus love the people they deeply desire to love.

One of the most significant qualities of humility is the knowledge that the small details of how we live together matter very much to love. Sometimes we hear people say, "At home you can be yourself," and they use this to justify their bad moods or to be rude and critical to a spouse and children who are "only family." Humility is always attentive to the feelings of the near and dear as well as of those we do not know. Humility knows that for love to flourish and grow, courtesy must be particularly exercised with those with whom we share our lives.

I have a friend who lived in an intentional Christian community with her husband and children for several years. When I asked her later why she left, she said that she had gotten tired living with people who believed that the essence of serious Christian friendship was having deep, heartfelt conversations at the dinner table, where everyone bared their hearts, while no one but her ever attended to taking out the garbage. I still hear her voice saying, "I thought taking out the garbage was an act of Christian love!" Many couples who start out good companions to each other founder over this point as one or the other decides she or he has work to do more significant than sharing the daily household chores. Often he or she is shocked at the "pettiness" of the other person, who put so much stock in sharing these humble details. Marriage is not the only kind of community of love where this problem arises. It is not uncommon to see deep resentment in churches on just this point of unequally shared work.[16] This funny story from the desert shows us that it was a problem in the ancient monastic community as well:

> It was said of Abba John the Dwarf, that one day he said to his elder brother, "I should like to be free of all care, like the angels, who do not work, but ceaselessly offer worship to God." So he took off his cloak and went away into the desert. After a week he came back to his brother. When he knocked at the door, he heard his brother say, before he opened it, "Who are you?" He said, "I am John, your brother." But he replied, "John has become an angel, and henceforth he is no longer among [human beings]." The other begged him saying, "It is I." However, his brother did not let him in, but left him there in distress until morning. Then, opening the door, he said to him, "You are a man and you must once again work in order to eat." Then John made a prostration before him, saying, "Forgive me."[17]

Another characteristic of humility is its abandonment of purity as the main goal of the Christian life. In deciding whether to associate with certain "known sinners," many Christians spend a lot of time trying to be above reproach. Others who would do some good for other people worry about whether their own motives for charity are pure enough to count.

> A brother said to Abba Poemen, "If I give my brother a little bread or something else, the demons tarnish these gifts saying it was only done

to please [people]." The old man said to him, "Even if it is to please [people], we must give the brother what he needs."[18]

Humility gives up such worries to focus on the real needs of real people.

How do we pursue the virtue of humility? We may begin by meditating in prayer on the real nature of humility. The use of Scripture is particularly helpful. Ponder in God's presence, for example, the meaning of the great hymn of Philippians in praise of God's own humility in Christ.[19] Think about how that humility was revealed in Jesus' concern for the most "insignificant" and ordinary people. Consider his lack of interest in maintaining his own reputation as being above reproach. Ask yourself where your own expectations about how you relate to others are in conflict with the patterns of humility. Ask God for help. Then remember the monastic advice that we not act against what we pray for.

DISCERNMENT

Discernment is the virtue of exercising our Christian intelligence in our desire to love.

> Abba Poemen said that Abba Ammonas said, "A man can spend his whole time carrying an axe without succeeding in cutting down the tree; while another, with experience of tree-felling brings the tree down with a few blows. He said that the axe is discernment."[20]

For many people this is very hard. They would prefer to have a list of what Christians must do or not do and then apply the rule in every case. The search for simplicity is not the route to Christian love.

Always we must consider what effect our maintaining our principles will have on others and whether we really want to be responsible for the consequences of being unbending with respect to our principles. Thus we have this shocking piece of monastic advice: One day Abba Alonius was asked,

> "How can I control my tongue so as to tell no more lies?" Abba Alonius said to him, "If you do not lie, you prepare many sins for yourself." "How is that?" said he. The old man said to him, "Suppose two men have committed a murder before your eyes and one of them fled to your

cell. The magistrate, seeking him, asks you, 'Have you seen the murderer?' If you do not lie, you will deliver that man to death. It is better for you to abandon him unconditionally to God, for [God] knows all things."[21]

In this case to turn the murderer over to the police was to turn him over to immediate execution. According to the desert teachers, however, only God can make such a decision.

Consider also this case from the Egyptian desert:

A brother came to see Abba Poemen and said to him, "I sow my field and give away in charity what I reap from it." The old man said to him, "That is good," and he departed with fervour and intensified his charity. Hearing this, Abba Anoub said to Abba Poemen, "Do you not fear God, that you have spoken like that to the brother?" The old man remained silent. Two days later Abba Poemen saw the brother coming and in the presence of Abba Anoub said to him, "What did you ask me the other day? I was not attending." The brother said, "I said that I sow my field and give away what I gain in charity." Abba Poemen said to him, "I thought you were speaking of your brother who is in the world. If it is you who are doing this, it is not right for a monk." At these words the brother was saddened and said, "I do not know any other work and I cannot help sowing the fields." When he had gone away, Abba Anoub made a prostration and said, "Forgive me." Abba Poemen said, "From the beginning I too knew it was not the work of a monk but I spoke as I did, adapting myself to his ideas and so I gave him courage to increase his charity. Now he has gone away full of grief and yet he will go on as before."[22]

Abba Anoub's distress over Poemen's original advice to the farmer-monk stemmed from his convictions about what behavior was and was not suitable for monks. Poemen taught him instead that if love is the goal of the life he wanted to live, he must not just expect to live by principles. Love is not about maintaining an ideology. God made us different and deals with us differently. This means that part of the exercise of discernment is always going to entail careful, close listening to the people with whom we live. Parents of more than one child know that while it may be admirable to try to treat all siblings alike from the standpoint of principle, in actual fact what is good for one child may do serious harm to another. Children are different from each other in disposition, abilities, interests, ways of seeing, stamina, and intelligence, and love must take these differences into account.

From the community of marriage to the community of our world, if we truly wish to live together in the kind of love the Abbas and Ammas help us envision, we need to grow into the virtue of discernment. Apart from deliberately trying our best to determine what the always-specific needs of love are, we can ponder Jesus' careful listening to the people he desired to heal, from the woman at the well to the man whose son was possessed by a demon the disciples could not cast out. In our prayer we can ask God for trust that we do not need to be able to know the answers to every situation in advance. We can also ask for help in being able to be realistic in our expectations of other people.

CONSULTATION

The monastics assumed (as we should expect from Dorotheos's circle) that from the beginning of the Christian life to its end we are deeply dependent on fellow Christians for nourishment, growth, encouragement, insight, and opposition. We must continually ask for and expect to receive help from others. Consultation is the virtue that enables us to do so.

The original context of consultation was that of the relationship between the Abba or Amma and disciples, and the disciples with one another. The disciple was expected to reveal all his or her thoughts to the teacher for the sake of understanding herself or himself and making progress.

> It was said of a brother that he had to fight against blasphemy and he was ashamed to admit it. He went where he heard some great old men lived to see them, in order to open his heart to them but when he got there, he was ashamed to admit his temptation. So he kept going to see Abba Poemen. The old man saw he was worried, and he was sorry he did not tell him what was wrong. So one day he forestalled him and said, "For a long time you have been coming here to tell me what is troubling you, and when you are here you will not tell me about it. . . . Now tell me, my child, what it is all about." He said to him, "The demon wars against me to make me blaspheme God and I am ashamed to say so." So he told him all about it and immediately he was relieved.[23]

Apart from the encouraging advice and insight the teacher nearly always had to bring, there was something healing simply in sharing the burden verbally with the teacher.

Although a person stood in a special relation to his or her teacher, the monk or nun knew that he or she must rely equally on the other brothers and sisters for insight and advice. Recall the old monk who was not able to understand Scripture until he was willing to go to a brother for help.[24] We learn the Christian virtues from each other in a most fundamental way. Such learning is not optional; our very salvation depends on it.

> Someone asked Abba Paësius, "What should I do about my soul, because it is insensitive and does not fear God?" He said to him, "Go, and join a man who fears God, and live near him; he will teach you, too, to fear God."[25]

With consultation we also learn to bear one another's burdens and have our burdens borne by our brothers and sisters in prayer. A year or two ago a friend of mine was struggling to forgive her mother for some very serious injuries. Not only had she found that she did not really want to forgive her mother, she was not able even to pray for her. My friend takes the communion of the saints very seriously, and so she asked me and some other friends to pray for her mother for a time in her place while she herself tried to find a way to pray. Resting in the prayers of others, she was able finally to pray herself and find healing.

Independence and total self-sufficiency are not virtues of love in community. Dorotheos of Gaza was so sure of this that he actually said:

> If it is my duty to get something done, I prefer it to be done with my neighbor's advice, even if I do not agree with him and it goes wrong, rather than to be guided by my own opinion and have it turn out right.[26]

Although we might not want to go along with Dorotheos completely, his advice is good in marriage and in churches alike. Shared decisions in marriage, committee work in our churches, doing things by consensus all take time and are open to inefficiency and bungling. In no community of Christian love, however, is there place for their opposite: "If you want something done right, do it yourself."

It is within this context of mutual consultation that we hear other advice that also falls strangely on modern Christian ears. Abba James said, "It is better to receive hospitality than to give it."[27] Many people are raised not to be beholden to anybody. Not being beholden suggests not needing to owe anybody anything, not putting anyone else in a position of moral superiority over us. Not being beholden is not a Christian virtue.

Even apart from the question of being beholden, we must not think that love is something we do only for others. We must not forget that for love to be reciprocal we must make ourselves vulnerable to receive:

> Some old men were entertaining themselves at Scetis by having a meal together; amongst them was Abba John. A venerable priest got up to offer drink, but nobody accepted any from him, except Abba John the Dwarf. They were surprised and said to him, "How is it that you, the youngest, dared to let yourself be served by the priest?" Then he said to them, "When I get up to offer drink, I am glad when everyone accepts it, since I am receiving my reward; that is the reason, then, that I accepted it, so that he also might gain his reward and not be grieved by seeing that no-one would accept anything from him." When they heard this, they were all filled with wonder and edification at his discretion.[28]

Learning to receive gifts is as much of a Christian discipline of love as that of giving.

To grow in the patterns of consultation we must be honest with one another, as well as support one another. One form of love-destroying dishonesty characteristic of life together in our marriages and churches is our niceness. In our niceness we believe that being supportive means never speaking our real thoughts and feelings in areas of disagreement. I am not at all recommending that we be brutally honest with each other. Honesty never needs to be brutal and there are many admonitory stories from the desert on precisely this point.[29] If we are to love each other, however, we need to know what the people we love really think and not just what we think they think. Where we disagree, we need to push against each other in direct ways rather than in underhanded ways that usually result in mutual bitterness.

Dishonest niceness appears in another form in our Christian communities and works against consultation. Often we think that church is not the right place to share the darker, more ambiguous or even painful sides of our private lives. Thus we do not expect to talk there about our anger toward our children, our grief over the loss of a parent, our fear of pain and death when we are seriously ill, or anxiety about the loss of a job. Frequently we get across the message to others that we do not want them to talk about these things either. Outsiders and often our children who have grown up in our churches, may experience this reticence as hypocrisy. Mutual love cannot exist fully where we do not share our real lives. Although it can be extremely difficult, we must be willing to learn to do this work of consultation together if we are to grow in common love.

How do we pray toward this virtue? We can ask God to help us recognize within ourselves those attitudes and behaviors that work against it. We can pray to be released from the conviction that it is weak to need help from others. We can pray for the subsidiary virtues of patience and humility to give up the belief that we ought to have absolute control of our own spiritual destinies.

KNOWING OURSELVES TO BE SINNERS

Dorotheos of Gaza believed that the most serious mistake that Adam and Eve made was not their first, that is, eating the fruit. It was in their refusal to take responsibility for what they had done and say they were sorry. God came first to Adam,

> and said, "Adam, where are you?" . . . —as if urging him sharply to say, "Forgive me!" But there was no sign of humility. There was no change of heart but rather the contrary. He replied, "The wife that *you* gave me"—mark you, not "my wife"—"deceived me," as if to say, "this is the disaster you placed upon my head." So it is, my brethren, when a man has not the guts to accuse himself [or herself], [that person] does not scruple to accuse God, [Godself]. Then God came to Eve and said to her, "Why did you not keep the command I gave you?" as if saying, "If you would only say, 'Forgive me.' " . . . And again, not a word! No "forgive me." She only answered, "The serpent deceived me!"—as if to say, if the serpent did wrong, what concern is that to me? What are you doing, you wretches? Kneel in repentance, acknowledge your fault, take pity on your nakedness. But neither the one nor the other stooped to self-accusation, no trace of humility was found in either of them. And now look and consider how this was only an anticipation of our own state![30]

Progress in any area of our lives depends upon taking responsibility for ourselves before God.[31]

Just as fundamental as taking responsibility for ourselves before God is taking responsibility before one another. For the monastic teachers a life of love of the neighbor depended upon learning to see our faults, then admit them to one another and apologize. Otherwise our life together would go on under a terrible burden.

Abba John said, "We have put the light burden on one side, that is to say, self-accusation, and we have loaded ourselves with a heavy one, that is to say, self-justification."[32]

Where we cannot examine ourselves truthfully to find our own part in any breach with another person and then say we're sorry, wounds are formed in us and in those we injure that cannot heal and that thus keep us from God and one another.

For many of us this admission is nearly impossible because when we admit a mistake, we experience it is a loss of self as well as a loss of self-esteem. We are thus apt to react self-righteously and defensively when the requirements of love would have us react in just the opposite way. As we saw in the last chapter, the beginning of being freed from this terrible burden is to begin to claim ourselves in God, pondering what it means to say that our worth as people is not dependent upon what we do, right or wrong, but rather on God's gift to us.

The passion that is the opposite of this virtue is judgmentalism. The necessity of giving up judgmentalism in all its varieties occupies an enormous space in the early monastic discussions of living in communities of love. Our ancestors were concerned about the many-faceted ways we feel called upon to claim our own goodness and our identity at the expense of marking ourselves off from and excluding others. Judgmentalism destroys community; it destroys those who do the judging, and, even more seriously for the monastic teachers, it often destroys (and certainly excludes from community) the one who is judged. On a small scale judgmentalism destroys marriages, families, and churches. On a wider scale it provides the major fuel of racism, sexism, neglect of the poor, and national self-righteousness. Judgmentalism for this reason as a breach of love is as serious as any other sin we might commit against one another. Thus Abba Theodore warns us always to remember that

"He who said, 'Do not commit fornication,' also said, 'Do not judge.' "[33]

Sometimes we hear it said that we ought not judge because it is only God's right to judge, which may suggest to us that only God is allowed the enjoyment of making others pay for their sins.

In fact what we know of God's love for us suggests that negative judgment, whatever form it takes, can only cause God pain.

> One day Abba Isaac went to a monastery. He saw a brother committing a sin and he condemned him. When he returned to the desert, an angel of the Lord came and stood in front of the door of his cell, and said, "I will not let you enter." But he persisted saying, "What is the matter?" and the angel replied, "God has sent me to ask you where you want to throw the guilty brother whom you have condemned." Immediately, he repented and said, "I have sinned, forgive me." The angel said, "Get up, God has forgiven you. But from now on, be careful not to judge someone before God has done so."[34]

Dorotheos, commenting on this very story of Abba Isaac, makes it clear that God looks at the plight of even the hardened murderer with far more gentleness and compassion than we are willing to exercise. It is only God who knows another person's history, circumstances, and internal struggles well enough to understand why anyone does what he or she does.[35]

Indeed, if we are to imitate God's love for us, not only do we give up our judgmentalism, by our own gentleness we make a space for others' healing. This is why

> They said of Abba Macarius the Great that he became, as it is written, a god upon earth, because, just as God protects the world, so Abba Macarius would cover the faults which he saw, as though he did not see them; and those which he heard, as though he did not hear them.[36]

What did the Abbas and Ammas mean by "judging"? Certainly they did not believe that one could rear children or be responsible for teaching others without exercising judgment and even discipline, as we see from the following saying:

> Abba Macarius went one day to Abba Pachomius of Tabennisi. Pachomius asked him, "When brothers submit to the rule, is it right to correct them?" Abba Macarius said to him, "Correct and judge justly those who are subject to you, but judge no-one else."[37]

Furthermore, although the monastics were sure that acting as judge was incompatible with the monastic life, they were certainly not advocating the end of the legal system.[38]

The first concern of our teachers were those overt acts of judgment designed to punish and remove an offender from the community. They were concerned to oppose the self-righteous belief that moral or doctrinal purity takes precedence over everything else, and the corresponding belief that good Christians ought to be God's police. I recently heard of a painful example of the sort of policing behavior the Abbas and Ammas worried about. In a church not far from where I live not only were the parents asked to leave as known adulterers; their innocent teenage children were removed from office in the youth group.

The Abbas and Ammas saw that overt exclusion is not the only form of judgmentalism that destroys sharing life in a community of love. Being critical, nagging, and complaining about each other in small ways can be just as destructive.

> A brother questioned Abba Matoes saying, "What am I to do? My tongue makes me suffer, and every time I go among [people] I cannot control it, but I condemn them in all the good they are doing and reproach them with it. What am I to do?" The old man replied, "If your cannot contain yourself, flee into solitude. For this is a sickness. He who dwells with brethren must not be square, but round, so as to turn himself towards all."[39]

Even in small ways being continually critical is, as Abba Matoes says, a sickness, and it creates sickness in those on the receiving end of it. Some churches seem to be particularly vulnerable to it, and members who later leave these churches may become virulently anti-Christian because of their experiences. Churches are not the only source of this problem, however. The trust, enjoyment, and love in many marriages and families have been destroyed by what is often subtle judgmentalism. The adult survivors of these churches and families often spend their whole lives seriously wounded by it.

Another more socially acceptable form of judgmentalism that is just as deadly to love is listening to and passing on gossip, and the Abbas and Ammas warned repeatedly about the need for "control of the tongue."[40] A non-Christian friend once taught me a very painful lesson in Christian love when I passed on a particularly juicy piece of gossip. "How can you say that about another person?" she said. If it is not true, you are injuring her by that, and if it is true, don't you know that the more damaged her reputation is, the harder it will be for her to change her behavior?"

How are we finally to be healed of our judgmentalism? Abba Matoes said,

> The nearer [a person] draws to God, the more [that person] sees himself [or herself] a sinner. It was when Isaiah the prophet saw God, that he declared himself "a man of unclean lips."[41]

Cultivating the virtue of seeing ourselves as sinners is a major source of healing the wounds of judgmentalism in our hearts. Seeing myself to be a sinner does not mean learning to say habitually, "I am no good." Such a state of mind, in fact, prevents love by making us feel powerless, dangerously vulnerable, and cut off from other people. Rather, knowing that I am a sinner means taking seriously the knowledge that we all do or at least are capable of terrible things. The monastic teachers were quite certain that it is not possible to love other people unless we understand at a very deep level that our human failings in the area of love put us all in the same boat.

Learning the patterns of this virtue is vital though it is not always easy.

> Abba Poemen said, "If a [person] has attained to that which the Apostle speaks of, 'to the pure, everything is pure,' (Titus 1.15) [that person] sees himself [or herself] less than all creatures." The brother said, "How can I deem myself less than a murderer?" The old man said, "When [a person] has really comprehended this saying, if [that person] sees a man committing a murder [that person] says, 'He has only committed this one sin but I commit sins every day.' "[42]

FORGIVENESS

In our lives together, closely related to the patterns of love that go with knowing we are all sinners are the patterns of forgiveness. Love cannot exist fully where we carry unresolved and unreconciled grievances. So fundamental is this truth that one Abba made it the whole of his teaching:

> Abba Poemen . . . said about Abba Isidore that whenever he addressed the brothers in church he said only one thing, "Forgive your brother, so that you also may be forgiven."[43]

Whether we find ourselves holding grudges against others over small things or carrying burdens of apparently justifiable unforgiveness for enormous injuries,[44] what we carry around unforgiven divides us not only from others but from God, and so from ourselves as well. Jesus teaches us to pray, "Forgive us our sins as we forgive those who sin against us." This, I believe, is not a threat so much as it is a description of how we are: Where we cannot forgive, we cannot be forgiven because we have rendered ourselves closed to God's healing mercy.

Why is forgiveness sometimes so hard for us? For some people it seems as though the power to forgive or withhold forgiveness is the only leverage they have in a relationship, and so to forgive means to give up power in that relationship. For others to forgive may seem weak, an injury to self-esteem. Sometimes people are simply embarrassed. Often, however, inability or unwillingness to forgive stems from mistaken ideas about what forgiveness actually is. One such idea is that if we forgive someone, we ought to like that person. This idea, however, is only another variant on the belief that if you are Christian, Christian love, including good feelings, should always flow spontaneously and completely. In fact it is often true that we may dislike another person very much while we are actually in the process of forgiving him or her. Even Evagrius Ponticus, one of the sternest of the Abbas said,

> It is not possible to love all the brethren to the same degree. But it is possible to associate with all in a manner that is above passion, that is to say, free of resentment and hatred.[45]

Some people cannot understand forgiveness or reconciliation except to mean going back into a situation where they have been hurt in the full knowledge that the person who hurt them will hurt them again in the same way. For them forgiving means trying to believe against all evidence that the alcoholic or the abusive spouse who has promised never to do it again at least ten times before really will stop this time. In short, for them forgiveness demands that the forgiver lay aside his or her perception of reality to deliberately perform an act of self-deception. To the Abbas and Ammas, turning oneself over to this kind of manipulation was not forgiveness.

Instead, forgiveness, as I understand it according to the Abbas and Ammas, is quite straightforward. It has two necessary ingredients. The first simply is not seeking revenge.

> Abba Poemen said, "A monk does not . . . return evil for evil."[46]

Time after time the Abbas and Ammas make this point. Forgiveness means giving up a desire for harm to come to the person who has hurt us, either at the hands of God or at our own hands, in this world or the next. In most cases giving up a desire for revenge is easy; everyone knows that "don't get mad; get even" is not a Christian slogan. In my everyday life if my husband forgets to stop at the store on the way home, I do not want to punish him by seeing him go to bed hungry. If my friend fails to do something she promised, I have no desire that someone else let her down to teach her a lesson. In other cases, however, where a person I dislike offends me or injures me, it may take some real work during and outside of prayer not to want them to pay for it in some way. In a few more serious cases, still, not returning evil for evil, at·least in desire, may seem nearly impossible.

Second, forgiveness means actually and genuinely longing for the welfare of the person who has committed the injury. Forgiveness includes desiring the wholeness of the injurer. In many cases, of drug or alcohol addiction, or spouse or child abuse, for example, this means using the virtue of discernment as well as we can to recognize and refuse to cooperate in behavior that destroys and prevents the wholeness of the other person or ourselves. A painful story in the *Sayings* describes just this sort of situation. Once at Scetis there was a brother who continually stole.

> Abba Arsenius took him into his cell in order to convert him and to give the old men some peace. He said to him, "Everything you want I will get for you, only do not steal." So he gave him gold, coins, clothes and everything he needed. But the brother began to steal again. So the old men, seeing that he had not stopped, drove him away, saying, "If there is a brother who commits a sin through weakness, one must bear it, but if he steals, drive him away, for it is hurtful to his soul and troubles all those live in the neighborhood."[47]

Wanting another's well-being is not necessarily wanting what he or she wants. It is wanting another to be able to live in the love God created us for.

A story illustrating both of these characteristics of forgiveness appeared in 1990 in the city where I live. Earlier in the year a man was brutally shot and killed by a group of teenagers who were trying to steal his car as he waited at the train station to pick up his wife after work. All the parties involved were African American. The entire city was outraged at the cruelty and callousness of the murder. Three of the defendants admitted their part in the crime, received relatively short prison sentences, and testified against the fourth. The boy who pulled the trigger never admitted his guilt, in spite of many other witnesses, and was given a very long prison sentence. The judge gave the murdered man's wife an opportunity to address all the boys at their sentencing. To the gunman the man's wife had nothing to say. This is how the paper reported her comments to the other boys:

> "I'd like to say it takes a lot of courage to admit your guilt. . . . [My husband] cannot be brought back to life," she told them in calm, reassuring tones. But the killing, she said, "doesn't have to be a stumbling block for the rest of your life. I challenge you to rise above this, to realize that God loves you and you are somebody. You can be better. I bear no ill will toward you. Your life can make a difference. We're losing our young, black men every day. . . . For your sake, for your mother's sake, make a difference. That's what I challenge you to do."[48]

The woman whose husband had been murdered by these boys had forgiven them. She did not want the boys put away for life so that they would pay for what they did; instead she wanted them "to rise above" the murder, to become good men, and to make a difference with their lives, to join the human community of love. The goal of human life is love in community. The Ammas and Abbas were convinced that if anything can bring another person truly to turn away from destruction toward a shared life of love it is the the experience of forgiveness.

This woman was able to forgive a terrible injury in an extraordinary way. But many of us are carrying around injuries that we cannot seem to forgive because they have ruined our lives. We may feel that our lives can never be set right from injuries our parents or other adults we trusted inflicted upon us as children; injuries from former marriages where our ex-spouse really wanted our harm and not our welfare; wounds our children have inflicted; crimes committed perhaps by strangers against us or people we love. Somehow the part of ourselves with which we might forgive seems inaccessible. Do we have to forgive in order to love?

Yes. We forgive not because that is what good people must do, but because it is what we need for our own wholeness and the wholeness of the people with whom we live who are on the receiving end of the unforgiven hurts we suffer. So how do we do it?

First, and often hardest, we must want to forgive. I believe that often when we pray for help in forgiving we are not able to receive the help because we have not noticed that we do not really want it. For some kinds of hurts to be healed we need to spend a very long time, perhaps months or years, simply praying to want to forgive. Although we may feel terribly discouraged, this is a prayer I believe God always finally answers.

Second, we need to pray to understand, if possible, the pain and brokenness of our wounders. Abba Poemen said,

> "Not understanding what has happened prevents us from going on to something better."[49]

It is not only what has happened in and to ourselves we must understand in order to go on to something better. In my prayer I can ask, "What is it in my mother's own childhood and adult life that made her so critical or made her an alcoholic? What happened to my father that has made him so cold?" I must be willing to listen attentively outside of prayer—to family or even to books and the newspaper—for information on injuries that would help me do this. At the same time I must try to enter imaginatively into what it must really feel like, even at present, to be in the shoes of my injurer.

Third, we can pray for help to see the consequences to others as well as ourselves of our lack of forgiveness. Is nursing the memory of injuries committed by my childhood family worth the pain my lack of forgiveness is causing my parents now that they are approaching death? Do I want to hold on to my continuing and unresolved resentments and insecurities at the price of the injuries I inflict on my own spouse and children, coming out of those old hurts?

Finally, we can and must pray every day for the well-being of our injurers. Anyone who has really struggled a long time to forgive the apparently unforgivable knows forgiveness is not a simple matter of willpower. As we have seen, the beginning of forgiveness may be months or even years of asking God for help in even wanting their well-being, but that desire will finally come. The ability to forgive is finally a gift of God's grace. As painful as this process can be, we will finally be able to forgive, for the promise is that in God, all things are finally reconciled.

Abba John the Dwarf said,

"A house is not built by beginning at the top and working down. You must begin with the foundations in order to reach the top." They said to him, "What does this saying mean?" He said, "The foundation is our neighbour, whom we must win, and that is the place to begin. For all the commandments of Christ depend on this one."[50]

As our monastic teachers have shown us, the foundation of our life in God is our life together. We will find in the next chapter how the desire for and love of God is both the ground in which that foundation is dug and its completion.

Chapter 6 _____

The Desire for God

*T*he monastic teachers have told us repeatedly that love of neighbor can never be separated from love of God. For this reason, in the two preceding chapters we looked first at what the Abbas and Ammas had to say about the need to claim our identity in God in order to enable us to love. Then we examined what love of neighbor means, as well as the patterns of love that lead to it. In this chapter we at last turn to our relationship to God and our prayer.

We began our discussion of prayer in chapter 1 with two images of prayer from the *Sayings*. The first, from Abba Joseph, is the image of flame:

> Abba Lot went to see Abba Joseph and said to him, "Abba, as far as I can, I say my little office, I fast a little, I pray and meditate, I live in peace and as far as I can, I purify my thoughts. What else can I do?" Then the old man stood up and stretched his hands toward heaven. His fingers became like ten lamps of fire and he said to him, "If you will, you can become all flame."[1]

For Abba Joseph, if they would, human beings can not only pray, but actually become their own prayer, mysteriously stretching out to and answering the fire of the Holy Spirit.[2] Thus the disciple who asks his Abba about prayer is told, if you only desire it, prayer can be for you the transformatin of your whole being in God, who calls you and ardently desires you to be as God intended you to be at the creation of the world.[3]

The second image of prayer, which appears to be just the opposite of that of flame, is associated with Abba Anthony. It is an image of the essence of prayer not as otherworldly and mysterious but as an ordinary, everyday steady round of humble routine:

> When the holy Abba Anthony lived in the desert he was beset by [restless boredom], and attacked by many sinful thoughts. He said to God, "Lord, I want to be saved but these thoughts do not leave me alone; what shall I do in my affliction? How can I be saved?" A short while afterwards, when he got up to go out, Anthony saw a man like himself sitting at his work, getting up from his work to pray, then sitting down and plaiting a rope, then getting up again to pray. It was an angel of the Lord sent to correct and reassure him. He heard the angel saying to him, "Do this and you will be saved." At these words, Anthony was filled with joy and courage. He did this, and he was saved.[4]

If you want life in God in prayer, the angel tells Anthony, do not seek it in high moments of intense experience. Do not expect it to come in extraordinary ways. True prayer is to be found in living an ordinary life of attentiveness to the very mundane world God created us for and set us in, in friendship with God.

How do these two sayings, which seem so opposite, relate to each other? As we might by now expect from our monastic teachers, they are not opposite at all. Rather, they are both together—flame and mundane work of life—the foundation of our relationship to God.

DESIRE FOR GOD

The root of all prayer, and indeed all life itself, is desire for God. All things are made to desire God. In the nonhuman, natural world, this attraction to God is what makes everything what it is: It is what makes acorns grow into oak trees; it is what makes lions roar.[5] Augustine said, at the beginning of his great prayer to God that is his autobiography, "Our hearts are restless till they find their rest in thee." Whatever the nature of our lives, in spite of whatever wounds we carry, as human beings we share in the blind attraction toward God with the rest of creation. Below the level of rational thought or choice, the desire for God operates within us, drawing us into life toward our completion in God, and whether we recognize it or not, this desire for God is the starting point of all prayer.

Once having made a beginning in a life of prayer, however, we find that where the desire for God formerly was unconscious, now it becomes conscious. Gradually what went unrecognized and was automatic becomes chosen. Our life in God comes to be a longing for God and delight in God's love that makes everything else without God seem empty and disappointing. Theodoret of Cyrrhus puts it clearly:

> When we weigh up against longing for the Master all the sorrows of life, we find them light indeed. Even if we assemble together all that is pleasurable and seems delightful, divine yearning, when put in the balance, shows them to be more feeble than a shadow and more perishable than spring blossoms.[6]

A little later Theodoret says the same thing in even stronger words:

> I prefer longing for the Saviour and Creator to all things seen and unseen together, but even if any other creation should appear greater and finer than this one, it will not persuade me to give love in exchange. Even if someone offers what is delightful, but without love, I will not accept it; even if he imposes what is melancholy, on account of love, it will appear to me lovely and utterly desirable. . . . I would not accept the kingdom of heaven . . . without the love . . . relating to [it]; I would not flee retribution in hell, if it was reasonable for one who has this love to undergo punishment.[7]

Fundamentally the desire for God becomes delight. Delight is the end of prayer.

> How precious is your love.
> The children of this earth
> take refuge in the shadow of your wings.
> They feast on the riches of your house;
> and drink from the streams of your delight.
> In you is the fountain of life
> and in your light we see light.[8]

Joy is another word for this basic desire or delight. This is why it was said that

> As he was dying, Abba Benjamin said to his sons, "If you observe the following, you can be saved, 'be joyful at all times, pray without ceasing and give thanks for all things.' "[9]

The saving joy to which Abba Benjamin referred on his deathbed was not a matter of keeping a smile on the face at all times.

Rather, it was a joy in creation itself, the same giving thanks to God, gratitude, and wonder of the psalmist who cries out to God:

Those who dwell at earth's farthest bounds
stand in awe at your wonders.
You make the sunrise and sunset shout for joy.[10]

Again and again the psalmist says, "I will go to the altar of God, to God my exceeding joy";[11] and "you make me glad by your deeds; at the work of your hands I sing for joy."[12] Joy or delight draws us toward God and each other from the very beginning of our life in prayer to its end.

One of the faces of this desire for God, this delight, is the joy of the resurrection. Desire for God is the knowledge that the world we live in is filled with the glory of God. Desiring God is to live "all flame" in the blaze of that glory. It is wonder at and enjoyment of a gift we receive that we never asked for or even imagined. It serves no purpose, and it leads to nothing except the praises of God, which are our love songs.

At the same time, however, the other face of yearning for God may feel not like joy at all but crucifixion. It often hurts as it draws us actively into creation, calling us not simply to desire God but to choose God in order to become the people God has made us to be. As we saw in chapters 4 and 5, this yearning can become excruciating as it shows us the extent of the psychic and spiritual wounds we would rather ignore than seek healing for. At the same time it summons us to seek healing for the wounded images of God we are, so that we may come to live in the new creation.

As we can see so well in the monastics' vigorous involvement at every level in their own world, desire for God opens our eyes and hearts to see and yearn for the healing of the world God loves. This means that it also pulls us increasingly into active involvement in the life of the everyday world.

Where does this desire for God come from? It is an image and a response to God's first delight in us. Sometimes we hear people say that the highest, noblest form of love is self-sacrifice, that because of the cross, we know that this is what God's love for us is like. The early church does not teach that the most basic quality of God's love is a suffering self-sacrifice. What first engages God with us is not duty or need or self-sacrifice or obligation or the need to be right or good but delight in us as beloved. As Dionysius says, God is:

> carried outside of [Godself] in the loving care [God] has for everything. God is, as it were, beguiled by goodness, by love, and by yearning and is enticed away from [God's] transcendent dwelling place and comes to abide within all things.[13]

Delight makes the lover extravagantly eager to make sacrifices for the beloved.[14] The cross, which is the occasion of God's own terrible pain, is very real, but it is God's delight in and desire for us that calls God to it. This is why the sixth-century writer Severus of Antioch could say that Jesus was crucified "in the divine cheerfulness."[15] Remember again the passage from the *Macarian Homilies*:

> A baby, even though it is powerless to accomplish anything or with its own feet to go to its mother, still it rolls and makes noises and cries, as it seeks its mother. And the mother takes pity on it and is glad that the baby seeks after her with pain and clamoring. . . . And she picks it up and fondles it and feeds it with great love. This is also what God, the Lover of [humankind], does to the person that comes [to God] and ardently desires [God].[16]

Delight is only a response to God's first desire for and delight in us.

Dionysius speaks of our desire for God as a great chain stretching between us and God to draw us to God's own self.

> Imagine a great shining chain hanging downward from the heights of heaven to the world below. We grab hold of it with one hand and then another, and we seem to be pulling it down to us. Actually, it is already there on the heights and down below and instead of pulling it to us we are being lifted upward to that brilliance above, to the dazzling light [of God.][17]

However anxious we may be about our ability to reach God in prayer, because God is drawing us always to God's own self, we know that:

> "If we seek God, [God] will show [Godself] to us, and if we keep [God], [God] will remain close to us."[18]

FRIENDSHIP WITH GOD

Closely allied to the active images of desire, delight, and yearning for God in early Christian literature are images of friendship
with God. The great second-century writer Irenaeus had said that
God originally created human beings to be God's companions,[19]
and it made a deep impression on some of our Christian teachers
that the Bible itself speaks of the patriarchs as "friends of God."[20]
If we also want to be friends with God, it will be helpful for us and
our own relationship to God to look at the characteristics of friendship we find in this literature to apply to our own prayer. These
include wanting the same things; freedom of speech and lack of
fear; holding each other accountable; mutuality of need.

First, friends want the same things. According to Theodoret,
"this is the definition of friendship: liking and hating the same
things."[21] By this Theodoret does not mean a superficial sharing of
tastes, that friends eat the same food or enjoy the same sports.
Theodoret is talking about something much more serious. Although
it is very important to friendship, in fact, he is talking about even
more than the necessity of friends sharing common values. Two
people can agree that friendship depends upon honesty, kindness,
generosity, and openness and still not be truly friends. Real friends
of the sort whose lives are inextricably bound together in love,
Theodoret believes, must share themselves in such a way that the
well-being of the one depends upon the fulfillment of the deepest
longings of the other.

For Theodoret our friendship with God calls us to such an
intimate relationship of love with God that our own happiness is
bound up with the fulfillment of God's deepest desires. Thus, he
says,

> The friend of God despises everything else and looks at the Beloved
> alone. [That one] puts serving [God] before all the rest together; [that
> one] says, performs, and thinks only those things that please and serve
> the One he [or she] loves, and abominates everything that [the Beloved]
> forbids.[22]

But what, then, does the Beloved desire? God's deepest desires are
for the healing and well-being of all creation. With respect to our
prayer, this is why Abba Zeno said,

"If a [person] wants God to hear his [or her] prayer quickly, then before [that person] prays for anything else, even his [or her] own soul, when he [or she] stands and stretches out his [or her] hands towards God, [that person] must pray with all his [or her] heart for his [or her] enemies. Through this action God will hear everything that [the person] asks."[23]

Zeno, of course, is not talking about a magical process here, by which if we pray in the right way, God will give us what we ask. If becoming friends of God means we are to love what God loves, we need to bear in mind that God loves people. If we desire to become all flame, we must also come to yearn for the things God yearns for, including the well-being of the people with whom, left to ourselves, we would rather not share the kingdom.

Second, friends speak their minds to each other openly, fully, and without fear. Of course it is not only possible but sometimes necessary to be friends with someone and not tell her or him everything we have on our minds.[24] In fact one of the most brutal acts people commit against each other is insisting on telling each other in the name of love exactly what they think of the other. Such truthfulness usually does no good either to the other person or to the relationship.

Nevertheless, on subjects that have to do with the very shape and condition of the relationship, friends cannot withhold their true feelings, thoughts, desires, and expectations from each other and still maintain the strength and truthfulness of that relationship. The woman who tries to keep her hurts to herself when she is continually angered and humiliated by her friend's consistent lateness when they get together is not the only one to suffer in the relationship. The tardy friend is being injured by not even knowing that she is destroying the relationship. The husband who suffers in silence at interminable parties his wife carries him to when he really needs to rest is by his stance of silent martyr seriously undermining his marriage. He is developing a grudge against his wife to which he is not allowing his wife to respond. Where there is genuine love and friendship, people must speak their minds and listen to each other.

What is true in our human friendships is also true in friendship with God with respect to our prayer. On the one hand, as we saw in chapter 3, God must be given a chance to speak to us and have us listen.[25] On the other, it is imperative that we speak our true minds to God. This means that when we pray we do not worry about the suitability of our prayer. We do not concern ourselves with wondering if what we are praying for is unworthy of God's attention, and we do not worry about being respectful. We tell God what we carry in our hearts, and we ask God for what we need for ourselves and for others, not to make ourselves feel better but because our friendship with God needs it.

> Abraham, Abbas Sisoes' disciple, was tempted one day by the devil and the old man saw that he had given way. Standing up, he stretched his hands toward heaven, saying, "God, whether you will, or whether you will not, I will not let you alone till you have healed him," and immediately the brother was healed.[26]

This kind of honesty in any relationship is difficult to come by, and it takes a great deal of energy and trust to maintain. The Abbas and Ammas were aware that this true freedom of speech with God does not come easily. Oddly, in seeking it they did not advise their disciples to screw up their courage to be bold and daring. Instead they invoked the first principle of friendship:

> Abba Theodore of Pherme asked Abba Pambo, "Give me a word." With much difficulty he said to him, "Theodore, go and have pity on all, for through pity, one finds freedom of speech before God."[27]

The beginning of learning to speak freely to God is also to begin to long for what God longs for. It is to cast ourselves passionately on the side of all people, as we come to see the world through the eyes of God's deep compassion and concern for every creature.

Third, friends hold each other accountable. Sometimes we like to believe that if people really love each other, they accept everything and expect nothing of each other. Real friends, however, expect a lot of each other. Each expects not only faithfulness to the friendship; each expects the other to keep his or her promises. At the most mundane level, if I share a vacation house with a friend, and we agree in advance that the chores will be shared, short of illness or another unforeseen reason, the relationship of friendship leads me to expect she will do her share of the chores. If she does not, our friendship depends upon my holding her accountable. At an even more serious level, people who love each other hold each other accountable to continue to act in character. When my teenaged son goes out for the evening in the car, I can expect that he will remain for the evening the same responsible, sensible, intelligent and kindhearted boy I know. If he does not, my love for him and his love for me compels me to hold him accountable for the character he should have shown.

Christians who live with an ongoing sense of the love, goodness, and generosity of God often find it hard to find a way of reconciling that love with any talk of God's judgment. I believe this is because so many of us have trouble visualizing judgment except in terms of an enraged, hypercritical, and judgmental parent who will not tolerate disobedience to his or her authority. But judgment means something quite different if we seek God's friendship and wish to live in it. Whether we feel it as the pangs of conscience when we gossip or whether we know it as the driving pain that urges us toward restitution and reconciliation for the larger sins we participate in by virtue of involvement in our society, judgment is an act of God's friendship toward us as God daily holds us accountable to the friendship.

All this makes sense. Somehow, however, although we expect God to hold us accountable in our relationship with God, we believe that it is blasphemous or at least wrong to ask for accountability from God in return. But the real saints of the Bible, the very ones whom the monastics took as their models for friendship with God, show us otherwise. When the Israelites made the golden calf while Moses was on Mount Sinai receiving the Ten Commandments, God responded by deciding to wipe out the whole tribe of Israel. Moses, however, argued with God, saying,

> "Why should your anger blaze at your people, whom you have brought out of Egypt by your great power and mighty hand? Why should the Egyptians say, '[God] brought them out with evil intention, to slaughter them in the mountains and wipe them off the face of the earth?' Give up your burning wrath; relent over this disaster intended for your people. Remember your servants Abraham, Isaac and Jacob, to whom you swore by your very self and made this promise: 'I shall make your offspring as numerous as the stars of heaven.' "[28]

Thus in the *Sayings* another Moses, the great black Abba from the Sudan, held God to account for God's promises:

> It was said of Abba Moses at Scetis that when he had arranged to go to Petra, he grew tired in the course of the journey and said to himself, "How can I find the water I need there?" Then a voice said to him, "Go, and do not be anxious about anything." So he went. Some Fathers came to see him and he had only a small bottle of water. He used it all up in cooking lentils for them. The old man was worried, so he went in and

came out of his cell, and he prayed to God, and a cloud of rain came to Petra and filled all the cisterns. After this, the visitors said to the old man, "Tell us why you went in and out." The old man said to them, "I was arguing with God, saying, 'You brought me here and now I have no water for your servants.' This is why I was going in and out; I was going on at God till [God] sent us some water."[29]

God had told Moses not to worry about running out of water and then had let Moses run out when visitors arrived. Moses was a friend of God and so he did not accept this quietly but "went on at God" till God kept God's promise.

Frequently, far from holding God accountable, we hear it said that Christians need to learn to accept whatever happens as the will of God. Only in this way can we find true happiness as we "turn everything over to the Lord," obediently refusing to question God, no matter what the provocation. This is not, however, behavior that fosters love of God. I know a mother desperately trying to come to terms with the accidental death of her eighteen-month-old baby. Believing that it is blasphemous to confront God with the loss, she is almost beside herself with grief as she struggles to accept that the loss of her child was God's will. She cannot accept it, and she believes as a consequence that she is losing her faith not just in God but in life as well. Whatever truth there may be in the claim that Christians must be willing to accept whatever happens as God's will, it is not consistent with what either the scriptural or the monastic Moses teaches us about friendship with God. I do not know how God will answer or the shape that accountability will take, but I do know this: If this woman is ever going to heal, if she is going to be in friendship with God, she must hold God accountable in that friendship. She must pray to God and say, "You gave me this child and you told me to rear her as my own. I loved her and agonized over her with my whole heart, and now she is dead. I cannot bear it. How could you let this happen? What kind of a world have you made that this could happen in it?"

The last characteristic of our friendship with God is mutuality of need. Friends need each other, and God is not an exception to this rule of friendship. I realize that this is a startling notion for many Christians, for we have been taught that God, being God, by very definition does not need anything. Certainly the early monastics themselves would never use the language of need to speak of God. Nevertheless that God needs us and chooses to need us in mutual love is implied in the early church's language of friendship with God and it is clearly seen in Scripture.

Aristotle, in the ancient Greek world, which assumed such an enormous social inequality between men and women, had denied that men and women could be friends with each other in the same way men could be friends with men. The highest form of friendship, he said, could not exist where there was not equality.[30] We know now that Aristotle was half wrong; in our modern world we have learned that women and men can indeed be friends. We also know, however, that he is half right: No human relationship can be described accurately as a friendship where one person is powerless and vulnerable while the other holds all the power, has no needs, and is invulnerable to hurt from the other.

If we speak of friendship with God, seen in the absolute, no human beings can be said to be the equals of God as God is in Godself. But Christians do not need to be in relation to God as God is in Godself. The incarnation has made it clear that God has chosen to cast in God's lot with us, becoming vulnerable to us to the very point of death. And God regards this as no disgrace but the very glory of the incarnation. This is why we hear these words in the great hymn of Philippians:

Make your own the mind of Christ Jesus:
Who, being in the form of God,
did not count equality with God something to be grasped,

but he emptied himself,
taking the form of a slave,
becoming as human beings are;

and being in every way like a human being,
he was humbler yet,
even to accepting death, death on a cross.

And for this God raised him high,
and gave him the name
which is above all other names;

so that all beings
in the heavens, on earth, and in the underworld,
should bend the knee at the name of Jesus
and that every tongue should acknowledge
Jesus Christ as Lord,
to the glory of the Father.[31]

The great story of Jesus' friendship with Mary and Martha, and his raising of their brother Lazarus, displays all the marks of friendship. As you recall from John 11, the story begins in Bethany when Mary and Martha call Jesus to come heal their brother, Lazarus, who is dying. With uncharacteristic insensitivity, Jesus does not go until Lazarus has actually died and been in the tomb four days. When he comes, Martha and Mary both confront him openly and even bitterly with their bewilderment and anger. Then Jesus, on his part, weeping in frustration on the hold death still has on life, raises Lazarus from the dead.

How is this story a model of friendship? Mary and Martha needed Jesus first to care enough about their anguish to come to heal their brother. Then when he did not arrive in time, they had a choice. On the one hand, they could withdraw into themselves in polite acceptance of Jesus' apparent decision not to come sooner. In that case they could have learned to live with unexpressed anger that would be a barrier between themselves and Jesus from that time forth. On the other hand, they could confront him with their rage and grief and disappointment for which they held him responsible. Fortunately for the sake of their friendship, they chose the latter. Jesus, on his part, because he valued their friendship, did not want them to speak to him in pious platitudes about accepting his will for their lives and the life of their brother. He was not trying to exercise power over them, and he was not concerned with their lack of respect. He needed and wanted to hear what they had to say to him, and he needed them to see his own frustration and pain at the power of death, whether he raised Lazarus from the dead or not.

Not only did he answer the needs of Martha and Mary. Perhaps it is actually because of the way these women chose to be even irritatingly faithful to their friendship in the matter of Lazarus that the real conclusion of this story was able to occur. John 12, the very next chapter, is the conclusion of this story of friendship: Mary's hearing and response to the deep need of Jesus in the face of his death. This part of the story occurs in Bethany at a dinner party that Jesus' friends, including Mary and Martha, held for him soon after the raising of Lazarus. Up to this time in the Gospel narrative, Jesus has frequently sought to prepare the disciples for his death, and repeatedly, to Jesus' frustration, they have refused to take him seriously. Now the time has come, and though there is no explicit mention in John 12 that Jesus is in mental anguish and loneliness over his approaching death, we know that he is, as we soon will see in the Garden of Gethsemane. One person alone in that room in Bethany, however, does acknowledge Jesus' need to have his approaching death recognized. It is Mary who comes in and pours over Jesus' feet a whole pound of precious perfume, to prepare him, Jesus says, for his own burial. What made Mary of all Jesus' followers able to meet Jesus where he needed her? I believe it was the same quality of friendship that she had expressed so passionately and openly in her anger at his failure to come sooner to attend her brother.

If we believe that Jesus who was truly God among us shows us what God desires of us, this story of the friendship between Mary, Martha, and Jesus teaches us a great deal about prayer and our friendship with God. God, who seeks our friendship, chooses to need us. God needs to speak to us and have us listen. God needs us to speak our minds. God needs to hold us accountable and for us to hold God accountable within the bounds of the friendship. God needs us to cast in our lot with God in such a way that what God longs for, we long for; what God grieves over, we grieve over; what gives God joy gives us joy as well.

INTERCESSORY PRAYER AND FRIENDSHIP WITH GOD

Private intercessory prayer is a natural expression of the friendship with God I have been speaking of. People sometimes object to the idea of private prayer because it seems as though it moves people out of the "real" world into a narrow, closed, and limited world. In fact the Ammas and Abbas would suggest that just the opposite is the case as we move increasingly into friendship with God. If friendship with God means wanting what God wants, as Theodoret says, then prayer moves us in spite of ourselves from a private world of love to a public world. There is nothing outside the scope of God's concern and love. Prayer brings us into the ever-widening love of all that God also loves, that is, creation, the people in it, and all that makes up our world.

Paradoxically, intercessory prayer does not merely follow from our friendship with God. We are actually enabled to grow in our friendship as we learn to pray for others. What happens in the process of forgiveness is a good example. If as friends of God we want to love as God loves, then, because they are dear to God, we must learn to love even those who have hurt us or who do not love us. Painful as it often is, as we push ourselves to ask God for help in desiring their well-being, our imaginations and our hearts are enlarged.[32] God truly gives us grace, and we find that what was begun with great effort and fear ends in a blessed and healing compassion. As our friendship with God has grown, so have the boundaries of our world.

Anthony, as the father of the monastic teachers, began his career in relative isolation from others. By the end of his career he found himself deeply involved in the life of his own culture. The last years of his life were spent seeing to a whole range of needs of all sorts of people, from the humblest to the most powerful.[33] Generals, peasants, pagan philosophers, archbishops all came for various sorts of help. In this respect Anthony is our model.

On the one hand, as we learn to pray in friendship with God, we find that we begin to deeply desire and ask God for the well-being not only of people we know or have some obvious connection with but for people on the other side of the world—people very different from us, from very different cultures. On the other hand, we also find our "close vision" improving as we become able to see people under our noses who before were invisible to us. As we begin to pray for the people we meet every day in the grocery store and on the street, we enter imaginatively into their world. As with new eyes we see people who are hurting for any reason, we no longer are able to say, "That is not my concern" or "If they are in trouble, it is there own fault."

What do we expect to happen when we pray in friendship with God for others? Everybody knows somebody who believes if you only ask God in the right way, "in faith," God will give you what you ask. Most of us also know someone who says, "I do not believe in prayer, and in fact I no longer believe in God. When my mother was dying, I prayed with my whole heart for her healing. I promised God anything God asked of me, if only she would be healed, but God let her die."

We hope to receive what we ask for, but we also accept that when we pray, we never know what the outcome of our prayer will be. We do not know the mind of God. There were more people whom Jesus did not heal in his lifetime than he healed. We do not know why some are healed and some are not. When we pray for another person, we often do not even know what they really need. To expect that if we only ask God in the right way or offer God enough in return, God will give us what we ask is to think of an act of prayer as magic or bribery rather than friendship with God. No one can manipulate or buy off God. If the starting point of prayer is friendship, however, there is not a friend in the world who always gives us what we ask.

Three things we do know absolutely about intercessory prayer as we face the fact that we may not receive what we ask in the form we ask it: First, whenever we long for and pray for the well-being of other people, we are only asking God for what God already longs for far more than we. Second, if we are to be friends of God, we must tell God what we want for others as surely as we must ask God for ourselves, without worrying about the appropriateness of our asking or the probability that what we ask for we will receive. Remember Abba Sisoes, who prayed for his disciple,

"God, whether you will or whether you will not, I will not let you alone till you have healed him."[34]

The point of this saying was not the healing of the disciple, which might not have taken place, but rather Sisoes's insistent asking. Third, where it is possible, if our prayers are to be true acts of friendship, we must not only pray for others, we must act in accordance with our own prayer. As Abba Moses said,

If a [person's] deeds are not in harmony with [that person's] prayer, [the person] labours in vain.[35]

If we pray for Christians in the Soviet Union, we learn about the needs of Christians in the Soviet Union, and we refuse to allow ourselves to regard them as enemies. If we pray for the poor, we must also take responsibility as citizens and Christians for poverty in the larger society.

Even having said all this, however, many good Christians long to pray for others and for the world and to have others pray for them, but when it gets down to it, they cannot believe that anything they could say to God could actually "change God's mind" about what will be. This was not a doubt from which the monastics suffered. As we have seen already, the Abbas and Ammas prayed powerfully and without reservation for those who needed their prayers. Wherever our concern about changing the mind of God comes from, it is certainly not biblical. In this chapter we have already encountered Moses winning an argument with God in Exodus, and we know the Old Testament portrays Noah and Abraham arguing with God on behalf of others as well.

If we expect to see what God is like by looking at Jesus, we must notice that in at least one significant case Jesus' mind was changed radically by a petition on behalf of another person. When Jesus was in the area of Tyre and Sidon a Canaanite woman came up to Jesus and shouted to him to cure her demon-infested daughter.[36] His disciples urged him to send her away, and he himself insisted, "I was sent only to the lost sheep of the House of Israel." When she continued begging, he told her, "It is not fair to take the children's food and throw it to little dogs." Quick as a flash with stubbornness and freedom of speech she responded, "Ah yes, Lord; but even little dogs eat the scraps that fall from their masters' table." Jesus, astonished at her boldness and her faith, commended her on it, saying "Woman, you have great faith. Let your desire be granted."

THE CROSS, THE RESURRECTION, AND GRACE

Being aware that the basic stuff of our lives is desire for God and friendship is one thing; living into that desire and friendship is another. The monastics knew very well that for most of us, if we are ever to become "all flame," we must spend a very long time dwelling in the smoke:

> Amma Syncletica said, "In the beginning there are a great many battles and a good deal of suffering for those who are advancing towards God and afterwards, ineffable joy. It is like those who wish to light a fire; at first they are choked by the smoke and cry, and by this means obtain what they seek (as it is said: 'Our God is a consuming fire' [Heb. 12:24]): so we must kindle the divine fire in ourselves through tears and hard work."[37]

For a good number of us, fear of, mistrust of, or indifference to God comes easily; if we are honest, love of God is another matter. For the early monastics proper love of self and learning to love the neighbor, just like prayer, are part of the ongoing work of a Christian's life, so learning to love God and to live out of God's delight is also the work of a lifetime. This is why

> Abba Anthony said, "I no longer fear God, but I love [God]. For love casts out fear"[38] (John 4:18).

The journey into intimate love of God is the journey into prayer in which, like Abba Pior, every day we make a new beginning.[39]

There are many reasons why learning to love God is a lifetime's work. As we have seen in chapters 4 and 5, one serious reason is the woundedness we carry that prevents love. That God has been a stranger to many of us most of our lives is another. While we can fear, be indifferent to, be fascinated with, and even infatuated with a stranger, we cannot intimately love a stranger in any real sense of the term, not even God. The development of any relationship into an intimate love that is a life-giving knowing of the other person simply takes time.

It takes time because real intimacy in any relationship is based on knowledge of the other person: Each of the partners must get to know each other's likes and dislikes, commitments, habits, work, values, moods, and history. If this is true in other relationships, it is true in a special way with God. If none of us can ever really come to the end of what we know about another human being, this is infinitely more true of God—so true, in fact, that Gregory of Nyssa actually suggests that heaven itself is an ever-increasing growth in the knowledge and love of God for all eternity.[40] Further, recall once more that the monastic teachers insisted that we come to know God only as we make God's characteristics our own through our prayer and our lives, sharing in the image of God. Learning the meaning of God's humility, forgiveness, and compassion by becoming ourselves humble, forgiving, and compassionate does not happen overnight.

Again, the long process of coming to know and love another person intimately does not occur on some lofty spiritual plane unconnected to ordinary life. If that intimacy is to be real rather than a fantasy, it has to develop within daily sharing of a common, ordinary, mundane life—the everyday routine sharing of chores, little pleasures, daily crises. Our learning to love God has to take time in the same way. This, in fact, is the meaning of what the angel taught Anthony in the saying at the beginning of this chapter.

It is true that "if you will, you can become all flame," but the Abbas and Ammas teach us that this only happens as we live in the ordinary world of prayer and work.

This mundane life is not, however, simply the dreary life of business as usual. The life of prayer, of growing into love of God to become all flame, is a process in which we learn to live in the power of the resurrection.

> Another of the old men questioned Amma Theodora saying, "At the resurrection of the dead, how shall we rise?" She said, "As pledge, example, and as prototype we have him who died for us and is risen, Christ our God."[41]

Life in the power of the resurrection is no simple and happy life, without complexity or pain. How did Jesus rise to be our pledge, example, and prototype? When Jesus appeared to Thomas after the resurrection, he did not simply show Thomas healed and antiseptic scars. To Thomas he said,

> "Put your finger here; look, here are my hands. Give me your hand; put it into my side. Do not be unbelieving any more but believe."[42]

Jesus rose from the dead in the joy of the resurrection, and yet he did not cease to be who he had been at the worst moment of his death. He rose with his wounds.

In much the same way, as we grow into the image of the resurrected Jesus, our pledge, example, and prototype, we also rise with our wounds. We, too, find that our resurrection in God is not a denial or disparagement of our wounds and vulnerability. It is not a sloughing off of our own past, no matter how painful and full of brokenness our past has been. The resurrection is not an abandonment of the cross but the incorporation of the suffering of the cross into the resurrection itself. As we bring to the life of prayer all that has ever happened to us, we find that nothing finally is wasted. Rather than casting off unwanted parts of our selves, we find instead that childhood pain, adult humiliation, experiences of joy, our own treacheries, confusion, loss—all are gathered in and somehow healed and transformed. We become able to look at our own past with love. Where we saw before only a wasteland of pain, now we see rich farmlands sown and watered by God's grace, bearing crops that become for us the very means of our love.

The resurrection does not take place, however, without our choosing it every day against our old ways of seeing and being. Jesus asks those whom he heals, "What do you want? Do you wish to be healed?" What apparently easy questions to answer yes! Unfortunately sometimes when we sincerely try to say yes, it happens that we have become so accustomed to our wounds and patterns we have developed for living with them that we cannot. The whole business of the resurrection seems too enormous. Like the rich young ruler to whom Jesus offered life, we find ourselves sadly walking away. Even here, blessedly, God does not leave us to ourselves. As Abba Pambo said,

"If you have a heart, you can be saved."[43]

Where we cannot hope, we pray for hope; where we cannot face the long and unknown road of the resurrection, we can pray for the desire to be healed. Abba Poemen was asked,

for whom this saying is suitable, "Do not be anxious about tomorrow." (Matt. 6:34) The old man said, "It is said for the [person] who is tempted and has not much strength, so that [that person] should not be worried, saying, . . . 'How long must I suffer this temptation?' He [or she] should say every day . . . 'today.' "[44]

How can this transformation of grace take place if our past is fixed? It is sometimes said that God is outside or above time. Whatever such a statement means at the theoretical level, life with God in the power of the resurrection means discovering that even the apparently immovable boundaries of time are fluid. Amma Syncletica said,

"Choose the meekness of Moses and you will find your heart which is a rock changed into a spring of water."[45]

If we only choose it, the rock of unforgiveness for hurts long past, the boulder of hurts we committed on others long ago, and the stones of attitudes and habits those hurts have produced can be transformed into life-giving, ever-moving water. Living in the power of the resurrection means refusing to accept that anything that is broken will ultimately remain broken. It is living and praying out of the hope and the knowledge that all things, within us and without, are finally reconciled and healed in God.

Because we share a common life in God in the communion of the saints, in some mysterious way this hope applies even to our relationships with those with whom we were not reconciled when they died. As we learn to pray for and with parents, spouses, old friends, all broken relationships are finally resolved and set right. But the scope of reconciling prayer and love is even wider than this. The church itself has been wounded and divided against itself over the centuries, injured severely by nationalism, fear of women, self-righteousness, love of power, and envy. For it and particularly for its teachers who both gave us so much and yet who have so wounded it and us, we also pray.[46] In the great prayer of John 17, Jesus prayed for his disciples and for all the disciples who would come after them into our own time,

> May they all be one,
> just as, Father, you are in me and I am in you,
> so that they may also be in us,
> so that the world may believe it was you who sent me. . . .
> With me in them and you in me,
> may they be so perfected in unity
> that the world will recognize that it was you who sent me
> and that you have loved them as you loved me.

The power of the resurrection is finally neither a simply personal gift nor a gift for the church. It is the transformation and reconciliation of the whole world[47] in the perfect unity and peace of Christ.[48]

The beginning and the completion of this transformation is in the God we love, who made us in God's image, who calls us into a common life with Jesus our brother, and who enables us to live it in God's own Spirit. This is the God who is closer to us than our own body[49] and yet more unfathomable and mysterious than the depths of our own soul to which we can never have access.[50] This is the God who orders the whole world with justice and beauty from the smallest part to the largest, the God "in whose light we see the light."[51] It is the God of wild grace, who delights in us, who for tender love of us in Jesus Christ has taken on all the darkness, pain, ambiguity, and vulnerability of what it means to be a human being in our midst. This is the God who calls us to our prayer, who prays in us, who draws us ever into love.

We come now to the end of the journey we have made together to talk with the Abbas and Ammas about prayer. Listening to them for one more word we hear,

> A brother said to Abba Poemen, "I see that wherever I go I find support." The old man said to him, "Even those who hold a sword in their hands have God who takes pity on them in the present time. If we are courageous, [God] will have mercy on us."[52]

Whatever the shape of our prayer, wherever or whatever we are or have been, we are never without the grace and goodness of God. We know that the psalmist describes our own experience of what has been and what will be:

> Blessed are those who dwell in your house,
> forever singing your praise!
> Blessed are those whose strength you are,
> in whose hearts are the roads to Zion.
> As they go through the bitter valley,
> they make it a place of springs;
> the early rain covers it with pools.
> They go from strength to strength;
> the God of gods will be seen in Zion.[53]

For those who long for God, who seek a life of prayer and love, every bitter valley at last will become a place of springs.

Human beings cannot make springs. All prayer, all life, all love finally are the gifts of God's generous grace that waters the world like the rivers of Paradise. In prayer we ask God for grace to enter the kingdom of love for which we were created. Prayer prepares us for the kingdom, yet paradoxically, whatever we do, it is always unexpected. Where we planted a little seed, we find an enormous plant. Where we mixed in a tiny bit of yeast, we find an overflowing bowl of dough. We come upon the kingdom as unexpectedly as and in more joy than if we were to find a treasure in a field. Praise be to God who in God's own self fills us with the riches of God's kingdom!

Notes

CHAPTER 1. "PRAY WITHOUT CEASING"

1. Macarius the Great 19, from *The Sayings of the Desert Fathers: The Alphabetical Collection*, trans. Benedicta Ward, S.L.G., rev. ed. (London and Oxford: Mowbray, 1981), p. 131, hereinafter referred to as *Sayings*.
2. Joseph of Panephysis 7, *Sayings*, p. 103.
3. Lucius 1, *Sayings*, p. 120. The Euchites mentioned here are sometimes called Messalians, and they represent a movement in early monasticism, especially in Syria, that appears to have emphasized prayer as an activity at the expense of work and the sacraments as well.
4. Part 2, "Of Quiet" 2, from "The Sayings of the Fathers" in *Western Asceticism*, ed. and trans. Owen Chadwick (Philadelphia: Westminster Press, 1958), p. 40.
5. In my previous book *To Love as God Loves: Conversations with the Early Church* (Philadelphia: Fortress Press, 1987), I attempted to share a good deal of their basic spirituality that has been life changing for me and that I have found has so much to contribute to our modern attempts to understand what it means to be a Christian and to live out that understanding. The present book builds upon the previous one, and although it is certainly not necessary to read *To Love as God Loves* to understand this book, many of the themes here, such as the passions and the virtue of humility, are treated in greater detail there.
6. Heb. 12:1.
7. Much in the *Sayings*, for example, suggests that regularity and steadiness in prayer is far more important than being in the right frame of mind, while Origen and Cassian both suggest that we do have to be in a "suitable" frame of mind for prayer, although they would also stress the importance of its regularity.
8. Examples include much of their advice on the amount of sleep we need, fasting, and the control of anger.
9. Dorotheos of Gaza was one of the most interesting and lovable of the early monastic teachers. He lived and worked in the sixth century in a famous monastery in Palestine, which was also the home of two other well-known monastic teachers in the ancient world, Barsanuphius and John, whose voluminous letters of advice are still extant. For a wonderfully readable collection of Dorotheos's homilies and a helpful biographical introduction, see *Dorotheos of Gaza: Discourses and Sayings*, trans. Eric P. Wheeler (Kalamazoo, Mich.: Cistercian Publications, 1977). This quotation is from *Dorotheos*, pp. 138, 139.
10. For a helpful discussion of the relationship of Justin and his contemporaries to the Roman Empire, see Elaine Pagels, *Adam, Eve, and the Serpent* (New York: Vintage Books, 1988), pp. 32–56.
11. For a full list of professions that disqualified a person for baptism at the very beginning of the third century, see Hippolytus of Rome's *The Apostolic Tradition*.

The relevant section can be found in English in Lucien Deiss's *Springtime of the Liturgy* (Collegeville, Minn.: Liturgical Press, 1967), pp. 137–38.

12. This is apparent from the very beginning with the letters of Ignatius of Antioch. Origen's *On First Principles* is an excellent third-century example.

13. For a detailed discussion of what can be known of early Christian prayer, see Paul Bradshaw, *Daily Prayer in the Early Church* (New York: Oxford University Press, 1982), pp. 1–71.

14. This seemed particularly true, for example, to the first writer of a Christian history, Eusebius of Caesarea, in his *Ecclesiastical History*. He was so enthusiastic in what he had to say about Constantine that it is almost a source of embarrassment to many modern church historians.

15. *Athanasius: The Life of Anthony and the Letter to Marcellinus*, trans. Robert C. Gregg (New York: Paulist Press, 1980).

16. Matt. 19:21.

17. Luke 10:27.

18. *Life of Anthony* 44, p. 64.

19. *Abba* is the basis of the medieval *abbot*.

20. "The First Greek Life" in *Pachomian Koinonia*, vol. 1, trans. and ed. Armand Veilleux (Kalamazoo, Mich.: Cistercian Publications, 1980).

21. "First Greek Life" 4, *Pachomian Koinonia*, p. 300.

22. "First Greek Life" 23, *Pachomian Koinonia*, pp. 311–12.

23. Although, as monasticism spread, in many cases whole families would take up monastic life.

24. Arsenius 15, *Sayings*, 11. Arsenius, who had been a Roman aristocrat and a very wealthy man before he took up his new life in the Egyptian desert, had a reputation for sternness and austerity.

25. "First Greek Life" 27, *Pachomian Koinonia*, p. 314.

26. See, for example, the first part of Gregory of Nyssa's "On Virginity," in which he exhorts young men to forget marriage and take up the monastic life. His argument in this part boils down essentially to this: if you marry, you can look forward to continual worry about your wife dying in childbirth, and if she survives, you will worry about dangers to your children. In *Saint Gregory of Nyssa: Ascetical Works*, trans. Virginia Woods Callahan (Washington, D.C.: Catholic University of America Press, 1967), pp. 12–26.

27. "First Greek Life" 32, *Pachomian Koinonia*, pp. 318, 319.

28. For a collection of texts by and about both Christian and non-Christian women in the ancient world, see *Maenads, Martyrs, Matrons, Monastics: A Sourcebook on Women's Religions in the Greco-Roman World*, ed. Ross S. Kraemer (Philadelphia: Fortress Press, 1988).

29. Palladius draws particularly interesting pictures of the way in which monastic men and women interacted with each other as equals.

30. Agathon 19, *Sayings*, p. 23.

31. The Messalians, or the Euchites (the first is the Syriac name, the second, the Greek), a movement within Syrian monasticism that was accused of stressing private prayer at the expense of the sacraments, may have been an exception. See p. 7 for a story from the *Sayings* concerning these people.

32. See p. 20.

33. It is significant that the first Pachomian community, in the absence of another church, even staffed a church for local peasants in its area for the recitation of the daily offices. "First Greek Life" 29, *Pachomian Koinonia*, p. 316.

34. Anthony 1, *Sayings* pp. 1–2.

35. For an account of a conversation on this subject, see Epiphanius 3, *Sayings*, p. 57. For a discussion of the rise of the daily office in the early church, see

Bradshaw, *Daily Prayer in the Early Church*, chaps. 4 and 7, pp. 93–110 and 124–49.

36. Moses 13, *Sayings*, p. 141.
37. See, for example, Arsenius 33, *Sayings*, p. 131.
38. Agathon 9, *Sayings*, pp. 21–22.
39. This is a major topic of a collection of his sayings in "Chapters on Prayer," in Evagrius Ponticus, *The Praktikos: Chapters on Prayer*, trans. John Bamberger (Spencer, Mass.: Cistercian Publications, 1970).
40. Macarius the Great 19, *Sayings*, p. 131.
41. Evagrius Ponticus, *Praktikos* 69, p. 35.
42. *Origen: Prayer; Exhortation to Martyrdom*, trans. John O'Meara (New York: Newman Press, 1954), pp. 15–140.
43. The most important is *On First Principles*.
44. In *Saint Gregory of Nyssa: The Lord's Prayer; The Beatitudes*, trans. Hilda Graef (New York: Newman Press, 1954). Especially useful are the pieces collected in *Saint Gregory of Nyssa: Ascetical Works*.
45. Evagrius Ponticus, *Praktikos*.
46. *Intoxicated by God: The Fifty Spiritual Homilies of Macarius*, trans. George Maloney (Denville, N.J.: Dimension Books, 1978).
47. *Pseudo-Dionysius: The Complete Works*, trans. Colm Luibheid (New York: Paulist Press, 1987).
48. See note 15 of this chapter.
49. Collected in *Pachomian Koinonia*, vol. 1.
50. *Palladius: The Lausiac History*, trans. Robert Myer (New York: Newman Press, 1964).
51. *A History of the Monks of Syria*, trans. R. M. Price (Kalamazoo, Mich.: Cistercian Publications, 1985), p. 83.
52. The relationships we see between the various monks and Theodoret's mother are extremely interesting. They clearly treat her as an equal in every sense, as she provides for them, comes to them for advice, and argues with them. There is no sign in Theodoret, as there is in so much other early monastic literature, that they found her femaleness threatening. See, for example, the account of her pregnancy with Theodoret in chapter on Macedonius, XII, pars. 16, 17, in *The Monks of Syria*, pp. 104–5.
53. John Cassian, *John Cassian: Conferences*, trans. Colm Luibheid (New York: Paulist Press, 1985).
54. The collection most frequently cited in this book is translated by Benedicta Ward. A topical collection is found in Chadwick's *Western Asceticism*, pp. 33–189.
55. Ammonas 3, *Sayings*, p. 26.
56. See chapter 2.
57. Part 9, "That It Is Right to Live Soberly" 27, *Western Asceticism*, p. 136.
58. Evagrius Ponticus, *Praktikos* 17, p. 58.

CHAPTER 2. LIVING INTO THE IMAGE OF GOD

1. Luke 10:27; Matt. 22:34-40; Mark 12:28-31.
2. Macarian Homily 46.3, *Intoxicated by God*, pp. 212–13.
3. Mius 3, *Sayings*, p. 150.
4. For one classic nonmonastic patristic statement of this theme of the image of God as a portrait that Christ renews in us, see Athanasius, "On the Incarnation," pars. 13, 14, in *Christology of the Later Fathers*, trans. and ed. E. R. Hardy (Philadelphia: Westminster Press), pp. 67–68. For an elaboration in Gregory of Nyssa, see "On Perfection," in *Saint Gregory of Nyssa: Ascetical Works*, pp. 109–10.

5. Macarian Homily 20.7, *Intoxicated by God*, pp. 133–34.
6. Poemen 67, *Sayings*, p. 176.
7. Letter 6, *The Letters of Saint Anthony the Great*, trans. Derwas Chitty (Oxford: Fairacres Publications, 1975), p. 21.
8. Part 17, "Of Charity" 2, *Western Asceticism*, p. 182.
9. P. 14. Dorotheos of Gaza, "On Refusal to Judge Our Neighbor," in *Discourses and Sayings*, pp. 138–39.
10. Serapion 1, *Sayings*, pp. 226–27.
11. Part 16, "Of Patience" 18, *Western Asceticism*, p. 179.
12. Ammonas 8, *Sayings*, p. 27.
13. Part 17, "Of Charity" 10, *Western Asceticism*, p. 183.
14. For a much more thorough treatment of the early monastic teachers' understanding of the passions and how they wound us see "The Passions," chap. 4, in my *To Love as God Loves*, pp. 57–77.
15. Where the differences are significant, I will draw attention to them in the text.
16. This list became the "seven deadly sins" of the Middle Ages.
17. Evagrius, *Praktikos* 7, p. 17. Note also that Athanasius portrays Anthony's first virtue as having as a child a lack of desire for variety in his food. *Life of Anthony* 1, p. 31.
18. It is important to note, however, how many scientists on the cutting edge of science now firmly believe that the observer can never take herself or himself out of the process of research in order to be "objective." Certainly most modern historians have given up the idea that the history they write is objective if one means by "objective" that the biases of the historian do not affect the conclusions he or she draws and even the questions asked in the first place.
19. Evagrius, *Praktikos* 11, p. 18.
20. *Ibid.* 20, p. 21.
21. The language of wounding is very common in this early literature. Anthony in his letters especially speaks of the passions as wounds and Christ as our healer; see letter 3, *Letters of Saint Anthony*, pp. 9, 10.
22. Part 17, "Of Charity" 18, *Western Asceticism*, pp. 184–85.
23. Isidore of Pelusia, 4, *Sayings*, p. 98.
24. Poemen 151, *Sayings*, p. 188.
25. Dorotheos, "On Fear of Punishment," in *Discourses and Sayings*, p. 188.
26. *Ibid.*, p. 188.
27. Anthony 35, *Sayings*, p. 8.
28. Nisterus 2, *Sayings*, p. 154.
29. Poemen 28, *Sayings*, p. 171.
30. Cyrus 1, *Sayings*, p. 118.
31. Evagrius 5, *Sayings*, p. 64.
32. "On Prayer," par. 17, in *Alexandrian Christianity*, trans. John Oulton and Henry Chadwick (London: SCM Press, 1964), p. 319.
33. "Of Patience, or Fortitude" 33, *Western Asceticism*, p. 92.
34. Poemen 11, *Sayings*, p. 168.
35. Macarius the Great 19, *Sayings*, p. 131.
36. Letter 6, *Letters of Saint Anthony*, p. 22.

CHAPTER 3. APPROACHING PRAYER

1. Arsenius 38, *Sayings*, pp. 17, 18.
2. Part 1, "Of the Progress of the Fathers in Perfection" 11, *Western Asceticism*, pp. 38, 39.

3. Cassian, *John Cassian: Conferences* 9.8, says, "Certainly, the same kind of prayers cannot be uttered continuously by any one person. A lively person prays one way. A person brought down by gloom or despair prays another. One prays one way when the life of the spirit is flourishing, and another way when pushed down by the mass of temptation," p. 107.
4. Evagrius, *Praktikos* 100, p. 41.
5. Not all Protestant traditions have quite the same difficulty with this problem. John Wesley, the founder of the Methodist movement which has blossomed into so many churches around the world, agreed with the monastics. He affirmed as one of his most important theological points that we do not earn God's love or any other part of God's salvation. Nevertheless he also insisted that human beings have both the ability and the need to respond to God's grace, for grace never overwhelms us, forcing us to do or to be what we do not choose ourselves.
6. Poemen 2, *Sayings*, p. 141.
7. Evagrius, *Praktikos* 100, p. 41.
8. Rom. 8:26, 27.
9. Evagrius, *Praktikos* 58, p. 64.
10. Part 11, "That It Is Right to Live Soberly" 1, *Western Asceticism*, p. 131.
11. Part 14, "Of Humility" 71, *Western Asceticism*, p. 171.
12. Part 10, "On Discretion" 98, *Western Asceticism*, p. 128.
13. *Life of Anthony* 25, p. 50.
14. Part 7, "Of Patience or Fortitude" 40, *Western Asceticism*, pp. 93, 94.
15. Poemen 36, *Sayings*, p. 172.
16. Chap. 5, p. 107; chap. 6, p. 124.
17. Part 7, "Of Patience or Fortitude" 30, *Western Asceticism*, p. 91.
18. Part 5, "Of Lust" 28, *Western Asceticism*, p. 68.
19. See chap. 3, above, pp. 61.
20. Epiphanius 11, *Sayings*, p. 58.
21. Poemen 183, *Sayings*, pp. 192–93.
22. "Letter to Marcellinus" 12, in *Life of Anthony*, p. 111.
23. Ibid.
24. Ibid. 13, p. 112.
25. Ps. 72:12-14.
26. Although precise methods of meditating on Scripture grew up in the Middle Ages and are often recommended today, there were no such well-defined methods in the early church. One book that includes a description of different well-defined types of meditation on Scripture that many people find helpful is *Prayer and Temperament: Different Prayer Forms for Different Personality Types*, by Chester P. Michael and Marie C. Norrisey (Charlottesville, Va.: The Open Door, 1984).
27. Note that Paul also makes this assumption about Scripture. In Rom. 9 he interprets the Jacob and Esau story; in Galatians 4:21—5:1, the meaning of Sarah and Hagar for the church.
28. Macarian Homily 11, *Intoxicated by God*, pp. 80, 81.
29. John 10:10.
30. See, for example, Gregory's "On Perfection" in which he lists nearly forty names for Christ from Paul's letters and the Epistle to the Hebrews alone. In *Saint Gregory of Nyssa: Ascetical Works*, pp. 96–97.
31. For the most influential patristic exposition of both how the names of God function in the spiritual life and how finally God is beyond naming, see Dionysius the Pseudo-Areopagite, "The Divine Names" in *Pseudo-Dionysius: The Complete Works*, pp. 49–141.
32. Part 15, "Of Humility" 72, *Western Asceticism*, p. 171.

33. Agathon 15, *Sayings*, p. 22.
34. Evagrius's teachings on this subject can be found in "Chapters on Prayer," *Praktikos*, pp. 52–80.
35. Evagrius's *Praktikos*, 70, p. 66.
36. See Basil Pennington, *Centering Prayer: Renewing an Ancient Christian Prayer Form* (Garden City, N.Y.: Doubleday, 1982).
37. John Cassian recommends, "Come to my help, O God; Lord, hurry to my rescue," Ps. 69:2, in Conference 10.10, *John Cassian: Conferences, Western Asceticism*, p. 132.
38. Part 15 "Of Humility" 70, p. 171.
39. *Life of Anthony* 25, p. 50.
40. See especially part 15, "Of Humility" 73, *Western Asceticism*, p. 171.
41. Anthony 14, *Sayings*, p. 4.
42. Like Arsenius's, recounted in Arsenius 33, *Sayings*, p. 15.
43. "On Consultation," in Dorotheos of Gaza, *Discourses and Sayings*, pp. 127, 128.
44. Arsenius 27, *Sayings*, p. 13.
45. Sisoes 40, *Sayings*, p. 220.
46. Agathon 9, *Sayings*, pp. 21–22.
47. Macarian Homily 18.2, *Intoxicated by God*, p. 128.
48. Syncletica 6, *Sayings*, p. 231.
49. "On Perfection," *Saint Gregory of Nyssa: Ascetical Works*, pp. 121–22.

CHAPTER 4. "ONLY MYSELF AND GOD"

1. Anthony 9, *Sayings*, p. 3.
2. Alonius 1, *Sayings*, p. 35.
3. Judgmentalism; finding identity through what we own; claiming identity by exercising power over others and claiming it in terms of possessions—"I am what I own"—are among the other most significant ways that lack of a self manifests itself in the early monastic literature, which we do not have time to discuss here. Judgmentalism here is seen as a matter of being distracted from one's own purpose and identity by annoyance or even bitterness that other people might be getting away with living by less strenuous rules of the monastic life than oneself. It was often accompanied by a willingness to set the offending parties straight. This kind of judgmentalism put the self in danger, as Poemen taught: "Instructing one's neighbor is for the [person] who is whole and without passions; for what is the use of building the house of another, while destroying one's own?" (Poemen 127, *Sayings*, p. 185). Even the ordinary desire for everyday goods was a temptation to the monastic because he or she saw in it the danger of getting trapped in an addictive cycle of wanting something, satisfying the desire, then soon after finding another craving rising in its place. Soon, rather than the monastic being grounded in God and showing love for neighbor, she would come to believe that her whole identity was tied up in what she owned. Defending her property and protecting her self-image with others would quickly replace a knowledge of her true identity in God. This is why Theodore of Pelusia says, "The desire for possessions is dangerous and terrible, knowing no satiety; it drives the soul which it controls to the heights of evil. Therefore let us drive it away vigorously from the beginning. For once it has become master it cannot be overcome" (Theodore of Pelusia 6, *Sayings*, p. 99). So Poemen's warning, "Do not give your heart to that which cannot satisfy your heart" (Poemen 80, *Sayings*, p. 178).
4. Macarius the Great 23, *Sayings*, p. 132.
5. Ammonas 4, *Sayings*, p. 26.

6. Part 7, "Of Patience, or Fortitude" 33, *Western Asceticism*, p. 92.
7. Macarian Homily 19.2, *Intoxicated by God*, p. 128.
8. Anthony 16, *Sayings*, p. 4.
9. Agathon 9, *Sayings*, pp. 21–22.
10. Macarius the Great 19, *Sayings*, p. 131.
11. Poemen 183, *Sayings*, pp. 192–93.
12. Gen. 32:26-33.
13. Luke 18:1-8.
14. Arsenius 10, *Sayings*, p. 10.
15. Irenaeus, *Saint Irenaeus: Proof of the Apostolic Preaching* 12, trans. Joseph Smith, S.J. (New York: Newman Press, 1952), p. 55. See chap. 6, below. Jesus identifies his followers as friends in John 15:14-17.
16. Isa. 49:16.
17. Luke 12:19, 20.
18. Mark 3:20, 21; 31-35.
19. Luke 6:6-11.
20. Luke 7:36-50.
21. Matt. 10:34-36.
22. Luke 10:38-42.
23. It was hearing this story directed at him that brought about Anthony's own conversion to the monastic life. Matt. 19:16-22.
24. Luke 15:11-32.
25. Luke 9:23-24.
26. Gen. 12:1-5.
27. Exodus 3 for Moses' call.
28. Part 4, "Of Patience, or Fortitude" 11, *Western Asceticism*, p. 84.
29. Poemen 200, *Sayings*, p. 194.
30. Dorotheos of Gaza, "On Refusal to Judge Our Neighbor," in *Discourses and Sayings*, p. 132.
31. Agathon 9, *Sayings*, pp. 21–22.
32. Evagrius, *Praktikos* 50, p. 29.
33. Anthony 16, *Sayings*, p. 4.
34. Instructions Moses sent, Poemen 4, *Sayings*, p. 141.
35. See chap. 3, above, pp. 59–60.
36. Isaiah 1, *Sayings*, p. 69.
37. Poemen 189, *Sayings*, p. 193.
38. Poemen 48, *Sayings*, p. 173.
39. Poemen 155, *Sayings*, pp. 188–89.
40. Poemen 163, *Sayings*, p. 189.

CHAPTER 5. "OUR LIFE AND DEATH IS WITH OUR NEIGHBOR"

1. Anthony 9, *Sayings*, p. 3.
2. Anthony 35, *Sayings*, p. 8.
3. Letter 6, *Letters of Saint Anthony*, p. 22.
4. As we see in the "Life of Daniel the Stylite." The whole middle section has Daniel not only advising an emperor but even driving the emperor out of Constantinople until he gets in line. *Three Byzantine Saints*, trans. Elizabeth Dawes and Norman Baynes (Crestwood, N.Y.: Saint Vladimir's, 1977), pars. 67–84, pp. 47–59.
5. Macarius the Great 39, *Sayings*, p. 137.
6. Ammonas 8, *Sayings*, p. 27.

7. For more on love as a disposition, see chap. 2 of my *To Love as God Loves*, pp. 29–35.
8. Theodore of Pherme 2, *Sayings*, p. 74.
9. See chap. 2, above, p. 35.
10. See, for example, John the Dwarf's long list. John the Dwarf 34, *Sayings*, p. 92.
11. For several, although certainly not all, options associated with particular teachers, see Part 1, "Of the Progress of the Fathers in Perfection," in *Western Asceticism*, pp. 37–40. A reading of the *Sayings* suggests that what that master virtue was must have occupied a great deal of monastic conversation.
12. Theodore of Pherme 13, *Sayings*, p. 75.
13. Agathon 9, *Sayings*, p. 21.
14. For a much fuller presentation of humility, see my *To Love as God Loves*, chap. 3, pp. 41–56. This quotation is found in Macarius the Great 11, *Sayings*, pp. 129–30.
15. See, for example, Dorotheos of Gaza, "On the Building up of the Virtues," in *Discourses and Sayings*, p. 203.
16. I also recently heard a story of a child who asked the congregation to pray for his sick dog. Unfortunately the minister regarded this as a trivial and unworthy request, and let both the child and the parents know so.
17. John the Dwarf 2, *Sayings*, p. 86.
18. Poemen 51, *Sayings*, pp. 173–74.
19. Phil. 2:6-11.
20. Poemen 52, *Sayings*, p. 174.
21. Alonius 4, *Sayings*, p. 35.
22. Poemen 22, *Sayings*, p. 170.
23. Poemen 93, *Sayings*, p. 180.
24. Chap. 3, above, p. 66.
25. Poemen 65, *Sayings*, p. 176.
26. Maxim 9, "Maxims on the Spiritual Life," in *Discourses and Sayings*, Dorotheos of Gaza, p. 252.
27. James 1, *Sayings*, p. 104.
28. John the Dwarf 7, *Sayings*, pp. 86, 87.
29. Part 5, "Of Lust" 28, *Western Asceticism*, p. 68.
30. Dorotheos of Gaza, "On Renunciation," *Discourses and Sayings*, pp. 82–83.
31. See chap. 4, above, and Dorotheos, *Ibid.*, p. 83.
32. John the Dwarf 21, *Sayings*, p. 90.
33. Theodore of Eleutheropolis 3, *Sayings*, p. 80.
34. Isaac the Theban 1, *Sayings*, pp. 109, 110. For a reference to God's dislike of judging, see Macarian homily 15 *Intoxicated by God*, p. 96.
35. Dorotheos of Gaza, "On Refusal to Judge Our Neighbor," *Discourses and Sayings*, p. 133.
36. Macarius the Great 32, *Sayings*, p. 134.
37. Macarius of Alexandria 2, *Sayings*, p. 152.
38. The early monastics take the social order, and that it is given by God, for granted.
39. Matoes 13, *Sayings*, p. 145.
40. A United Methodist minister I know speaks of this as "stewardship of the tongue."
41. Matoes 2, *Sayings*, p. 143.
42. Poemen 97, *Sayings*, p. 180.
43. Isidore the Priest 10, *Sayings*, p. 98.
44. Actually the monastic teachers did not believe that there really was unforgiveness that was justifiable.
45. Evagrius Ponticus, *Praktikos* 100, p. 41.

46. Poemen 91, *Sayings*, p. 179.
47. Daniel 6, *Sayings*, p. 52.
48. Montgomery, Bill, "Widow Urges Teens to Improve Lives," *Atlanta Constitution*, (July 18, 1990): Section A, page 1.
49. Poemen 200, *Sayings*, p. 194.
50. John the Dwarf 39, *Sayings*, p. 93.

CHAPTER 6. THE DESIRE FOR GOD

1. Joseph of Panephysis 7, *Sayings*, p. 103.
2. The Macarian homilies repeatedly use the image of fire to describe the work of the Holy Spirit in us. See, for example, homilies 4.14, 8.2, 11.1, in *Intoxicated by God*, pp. 45, 68, 77.
3. I connect this saying with the sayings about the Abbas whose faces shone like Adam before the Fall or Moses after the encounter with God at Mount Sinai, Pambo 12, *Sayings*, p. 197.
4. Anthony 1, *Sayings*, pp. 1–2.
5. See, for example, Dionysius the Pseudo-Areopagite, "The Divine Names," chap. 4.12, 4.13, in *Pseudo-Dionysius: The Complete Works*, pp. 81–82.
6. "Epilogue: On Divine Love" 6, *The Monks of Syria*, p. 194.
7. Ibid., p. 195.
8. Ps. 36:7-9.
9. Benjamin 4, *Sayings*, p. 44.
10. Ps. 65:8.
11. Ps. 43:4.
12. Ps. 92:4.
13. Pseudo-Dionysius, "The Divine Names," chap. 4, 13, *Pseudo-Dionysius: The Complete Works*, p. 82.
14. It is significant that patristic writers repeatedly write commentaries on the Song of Songs as an allegory of God's love for us.
15. An odd but helpfully evocative remark. No English translation. Syriac in *Liber contra impium grammaticum*, ed. Joseph Lebon CSCO, no. 101 (Louvain, 1963), p. 183.
16. Macarian Homily 46.3, *Intoxicated by God*, pp. 212–13.
17. "The Divine Names," chap. 3.1., *Pseudo-Dionysius: The Complete Works*, p. 68.
18. Arsenius 10, *Sayings*, p. 10.
19. *Saint Irenaeus: Proof of the Apostolic Preaching* 12, p. 55.
20. Abraham is called "friend of God" in 2 Chron. 20:7; Isa. 41:8; James 2:23; Moses in Exod. 33:11.
21. Epilogue 21, *The Monks of Syria*, p. 204.
22. Epilogue 15, ibid., p. 200.
23. Zeno 7, *Sayings*, p. 67.
24. Remember Abba Alonius's warning against trying to live out of the policy that one ought never to lie. See p. 103ff.
25. P. 67ff.
26. Sisoes 12, *Sayings*, p. 214.
27. Pambo 14, *Sayings*, p. 198.
28. Moses' entire prayer is in Exod. 32:11-14.
29. Moses 13, *Sayings*, p. 141.
30. *Nichomachean Ethics* 7. According to Aristotle, the only way the inequality can be ironed out enough to allow for anything called friendship is for the lower-status person, the woman, proportionately to love the higher-status person more than the higher-status person, the man, loves the lower.

31. Phil. 2:5-11.
32. Macarian Homilies 18.3, and 19, in *Intoxicated by God*, pp. 124, 128–31. Dorotheos has a very helpful discussion of precisely how this works in "On the Building Up of the Virtues" in *Discourses and Sayings*, pp. 206-207.
33. *Life of Anthony*.
34. Sisoes 12, *Sayings*, p. 214.
35. Instructions Moses sent, Poemen 4, *Sayings*, p. 141.
36. Matt. 15:21-28.
37. Syncletica 1, *Sayings*, p. 230.
38. Anthony 32, *Sayings*, p. 8.
39. Poemen 85, *Sayings*, p. 179.
40. "On the Soul and Resurrection," p. 240, *Gregory of Nyssa: The Ascetical Writings*. The reason we cannot come to the limits even of knowledge of other human beings is that we are made in the image of God, who is without limit.
41. Theodora 10, *Sayings*, p. 84.
42. John 20:27.
43. Pambo 10, *Sayings*, p. 197.
44. Poemen 126, *Sayings*, p. 185.
45. Syncletica 11, *Sayings*, p. 233.
46. I am indebted for this healing insight to Father Robert Stephanopolus, who responded to the pain I felt at the way in which the teachers of the early church failed to value women by saying, "If you believe in the communion of the saints, then you must pray for them."
47. That Christians could see this happening already was a convincing argument for the truth of Christianity to early Christians. See Athanasius, "On the Incarnation," par. 52 p. 106 *Christology of the Later Fathers*.
48. Pseudo-Dionysius, "The Divine Names," chap. 11.3–5, *Pseudo-Dionysins: The Complete Works*, pp. 121–26.
49. Macarian Homily 11.15, *Intoxicated by God*, p. 82.
50. Macarian Homily 12.11., ibid. p. 86.
51. Ps. 36:9.
52. Poemen 94, *Sayings*, p. 180.
53. Ps. 84:4-7.

Index

149

Select Bibliography

The following English translations are all available to the modern interested reader.

The Letters of Saint Anthony the Great. Translated by Derwas Chitty. Fairacres, Oxford: Sisters of the Love of God Press, 1975.

Athanasius: *The Life of Anthony and the Letter to Marcellinus.* Edited by Robert Gregg, Classics of Western Spirituality. New York: Paulist Press, 1980.

Dorotheos of Gaza: Discourses and Sayings. Translation and introduction by Eric P. Wheeler. Kalamazoo, Mich.: Cistercian Publications, 1977.

Evagrius Ponticus, *The Praktikos: Chapters on Prayer.* Edited by M. Basil Pennington. Translation and introduction by John Bamberger, O.C.S.O. Spencer, Mass.: Cistercian Publications, 1970.

Gregory of Nyssa: *The Life of Moses.* Translation, introduction, and notes by Abraham Malherbe and Everett Ferguson. Classics of Western Spirituality. New York: Paulist Press, 1978.

"On Perfection" in *Gregory of Nyssa: Ascetical Works.* Translated by V. W. Callahan. Fathers of the Church 58. Washington, D.C.: Catholic University of America Press, 1967.

Intoxicated with God: The Fifty Spiritual Homilies of Macarius. Translation and introduction by George Maloney, S.J. Denville, N.J.: Dimension Books, 1978.

Pachomian Koinonia. Vol. One: The Life of Saint Pachomius and His Disciples. Translation and introduction by Armand Veilleux. Kalamazoo, Mich.: Cistercian Publications, 1980.

Palladius: The Lausiac History. Translation by Robert T. Meyer. Ancient Christian Writers 34. Westminster, Md.: Newman Press, 1964.

There are many collections of the Sayings of the Fathers which have survived from the early church, in Greek, Latin, and Syriac. Of the two collections I have used here, the Ward translation is from a Greek text in which the sayings are grouped together under the names of the mothers or fathers to whom they are attributed. The other text, translated by Chadwick, is in Latin, and the sayings are grouped according to topic.

The Sayings of the Desert Fathers: The Alphabetical Collection. Translated by Benedicta Ward, S.L.G. Oxford: A. R. Mowbray, 1981.

"The Sayings of the Fathers," in *Western Asceticism.* Selected translations and introductions by Owen Chadwick. Library of Christian Classics. Philadelphia: Westminster Press, 1958.